UNDERSTANDING
THE PRIMARY
CURRICULUM

DATE			

UNDERSTANDING THE PRIMARY CURRICULUM

John Boyd

HUTCHINSON

London Melbourne Sydney Auckland Johannesburg

Hutchinson & Co. (Publishers) Ltd

An imprint of the Hutchinson Publishing Group

17–21 Conway Street, London W1P 6JD
and 51 Washington Street, Dover, NH 03820, USA

Hutchinson Publishing Group (Australia) Pty Ltd
PO Box 496, 16–22 Church Street, Hawthorne, Melbourne, Victoria 3122

Hutchinson Group (NZ) Ltd
32–34 View Road, PO Box 40–086, Glenfield, Auckland 10

Hutchinson Group (SA) (Pty) Ltd
PO Box 337, Bergvlei 2012, South Africa

First Published 1984
© John Boyd 1984

Phototypeset in Plantin by BookEns, Saffron Walden, Essex.

Printed and bound in Great Britain by
Anchor Brendon Ltd,
Tiptree, Essex

British Library Cataloguing in Publication Data
Boyd, John, 1935-
    Understanding the primary curriculum.
    1. Education, Elementary — Great Britain — Curricula
    I. Title
    372.19'0941   LB1564.G7

Library of Congress Cataloging in Publication Data
Boyd, John, 1935-
    Understanding the primary curriculum.

    Bibliography: p.
    Includes index.
    1. Education, Elementary—Great Britain—Curricula—
Cast studies. I. Title.
    LB1564.G7B68   1984   372.19'0941   84-3835

ISBN 0 09 156880 0 cased
ISBN 0 09 156681 9 paper

Contents

List of figures

Introduction

This book is as much about teachers as it is about the curriculum since the curriculum is the medium through which teachers engage children in learning. Whatever form it takes and how it changes in a classroom or school will be decided by the ways in which teachers perceive and interpret their roles. Thus it is important in studying the curriculum to consider teachers' beliefs about the nature of education and how these are expressed in the personal value positions which are at the foundations of individual professional practice. Since teachers' classroom autonomy is an established fact in schools in Britain it is especially important to understand how their beliefs underpin their decision-making in classrooms.

There are considerable differences among teachers as to what they accept and reject both as good practice and as its theoretical justifications. In Britain, thinking about the curriculum has been heavily influenced by American thought and practice but this has been pervasive rather than an overt and unconditional acceptance. Planning by objectives, or what became known as rational curriculum planning, arguably the only developed structure for curriculum planning, has never been fully accepted in Britain, at least in its more extreme behavioural form. Indeed, there was outright suspicion and rejection of this view of planning when it was first encountered by teachers and other educationalists in the 1960s, documented for instance by Maclure (1968a)* and in the equivocal treatment of the aims of primary education in the Plowden Report.

* Full references are contained in the Bibliography beginning on p. 178.

While the notion of objectives acting as guidelines to denote the range of concepts and skills which teachers should have in mind when planning their work has been broadly, if tentatively, accepted by teachers, behavioural objectives which seek to specify in advance what children will learn as a result of experiencing a lesson or a scheme have in effect been rejected as a basis for planning. A good example of teachers' equivocal attitudes to such planning lies in the history of the Schools Council Science 5–13 Project, the only example in this country of a large-scale project adopting a behavioural objectives planning approach. It was planned in this way largely because of the rejection by teachers of the earlier Nuffield Junior Science Project which was based on learning by discovery and avoided the production of anything that looked like a scheme or syllabus. In its avoidance of appearing to prescribe, its developers also failed to give teachers the kinds of assistance and direction that they were looking for in teaching science. Con- sequently, when the Science 5–13 Project team produced a draft list of objectives, the teachers in the trial schools were enthusiastic about them and were allowed to work with them. But after eleven years and three follow-up projects, Science 5–13 is still not used widely. Teachers' lack of science understanding and their consequent lack of confidence to teach science is part of the reason, but there remains a tension inherent in the project's design between the discovery learning-based philosophy informing the project team and in which learning outcomes cannot be specified in advance, and the use of behavioural objectives which require just that. Faced with this apparent contradiction, teachers tended to ignore or reject the objectives as being irrelevant or too complex or encroaching on their classroom decision-making responsibilities, but to accept the well-planned and presented source books which the project produced.

There is however a considerable amount of teaching materials and equipment which teachers use widely and which assume a degree of rational curriculum planning. The SRA Reading Labora- tory materials, Breakthrough to Literacy, and even graded work- sheets and cards embody assumptions about what children should learn through their use. But since the materials on the whole work well and their planning basis remains implicit, they are non- threatening to teachers.

This rejection by teachers of curriculum objectives, and perhaps the need to plan explicitly, can be seen as the expression of a more general issue: the perennial suspicion of theory and of theorizing about education which many teachers demonstrate. As Kelly (1982) comments:

For perhaps too long the assumption has been made by many teachers that education theory is for those who wish to talk about education, but of little value to those who wish to practise it. The gap between the theory and the practice of education has long been a yawning chasm and the rejection of theoretical considerations by many teachers has been total. *(p.1)*

He suggests that the obligatory educational theory components, however they are named, in teacher education courses are to blame for their failure to address practical classroom concerns and therefore to demonstrate their relevance to beginning teachers. This is important but a deeper source lies in the nature of teaching itself. To assert that teachers are mainly concerned with solving practical problems in classrooms is to state the obvious, but this might help to indicate the kinds of knowledge and understanding which they will regard as being significant rather than implying that all matters of theory will be of little importance to them. The distinction between propositional and procedural knowledge – of knowing that and of knowing how — is important here. While it has been claimed that teachers are concerned with the imparting of propositional knowledge, the dynamics of the classroom will place a heavy emphasis on the mastery of procedural knowledge in the form of knowing how to control and organize classes, plan lessons, motivate children, design and make teaching materials and record progress, for example. That the two kinds of knowledge are not mutually exclusive, and that propositional knowledge is a more elaborated account of procedural knowledge have important implications for the curriculum, as Pring (1976) has pointed out. But it is unlikely that teachers, having responsibility for the day-to-day learning of a class of children across the curriculum in a primary school, or for a wider range of pupils in teaching a subject in a secondary school, will see such a distinction as being more than just another bit of theory that cannot be applied.

It seems that only those bits of theory, usually introduced in educational studies' components, that 'explain' serious problems in getting children to learn, are taken up and retained by students and beginning teachers. Notable among these are Bernstein's theory of language codes, Piaget's stages in concept acquisition and Maslow's hierarchy of motivational needs. What is important is that they are all propositional, being generalizations based on research findings. When teachers adopt them to explain conditions and to justify their practices, a form of knowledge reductionism takes place, in that they become so closely applied to individual school and classroom situations that they effectively become procedural knowledge. There are inevitable distortions and oversimplifications when this happens. For example, a social pathology or deficit view of learning can be adopted by teachers which over emphasizes the categorization of children according to their predicted attainments and distances teachers from their possible failure to raise the level of attainment in a class.

Another aspect of this is the confusion between ideological positions and rationally defensible theories, the most notable in primary education being the child-centred perspective which argues persuasively, from psychological research and philosophical discourse, for the heeding of individual differences, the structuring of experiential learning climates and the integration of curriculum knowledge. Although child-centredness reached its apotheosis in the later 1960s it is still influential and pervasive. As Peters claimed in 1969, while the intellectual arguments for child-centredness have been won, the adoption by teachers of child-centred approaches has not been universal. Dearden (1968) has analysed such notions as children's needs and interests as they have a bearing on learning and teaching while Sharp and Green (1975) have identified the hidden messages behind the child-centred stance in one primary school. Again, it is the theory as rationalization that is dominant here, with a particular view of the child as learner in school and the proper role of the teacher in promoting learning being buried in the theorizing.

Given that teachers are concerned with procedural knowledge as the means by which practice might be explained, interpreted and justified, a fruitful relationship between educational theory and practice might be achieved by analysing examples of practice to see what might be generalizable from them. In doing this it might be possible to derive some conditional principles from examined practice which could be used initially to explore the complexities of teaching and learning and later perhaps to consider whether or not there are any general principles beyond the obvious and mundane which can be applied to teaching–learning situations. If traditional educational theory has so far failed to illuminate practice, it is argued here that the only theorizing that might make sense to teachers is that which comes from the disciplined examination of their own practice. By doing this, both the tools of analysis and the insights derived from analysis can be developed by teachers so that their practice can be refined through a greater understanding of its directions and complexities. Such reflexivity is a characteristic of Hoyle's notion of the teacher as an extended professional with all that this entails for individual teachers' expertise, articulation and accountability.

Hargreaves (1979) has considered teachers' decision-making in the classroom as an important focal point for developing understanding of the range of on-the-spot decisions teachers make through identifying the implicitly believed-in values which inform these. Teachers' own 'commonsense' theories embrace both their actions and their beliefs: by getting teachers to analyse their decisions, the links between values and actions can be revealed:

Values are imbedded in teachers' classroom practices; but because there is no simple correspondence between 'abstract' values and everyday practice, it is a research task to analyse precisely how values are, often tacitly, imbedded in action. Here is the significance of classroom decision-making, for it is in decision-making that all these features find their point of articulation.

My claim is that through an examination of the common sense knowledge, skills and values of teachers we can provide a basic model of teaching, and an important method of achieving this is through the collation and analysis of teacher commentaries. *(pp. 80-1)*

What is of general importance here is the possibility of deriving educational theory from the range of classroom processes embodied in everyday teacher–pupil interaction, and of such theory being fed back in order to improve practice. This could be done in a number of ways. First, there is Hargreaves's phenomenological approach. Second, there is the possibility of involving teachers in educational research so that research findings are both contributed to by teachers and fed back into their practice. The aims of primary education study carried out by the Schools Council and discussed here later is a good example of survey-type research where teachers were involved in analysing their educational aims through structured discussion, questionnaires and interviews. What emerged from this project was the way that fundamental beliefs about methods, organization and teachers' roles stemmed from the educational aims which teachers believed in. Third, there are a number of research studies into classroom processes, such as ORACLE, which consider different styles of teaching through studying classroom organization. Since teachers have been participant and non-participant observers in several of these studies, it follows that the results of their observations are likely to inform their own teaching performances. Fourth, there are the possibilities offered by teachers themselves engaging in small-scale action research projects of the kind which Nixon (1981) has documented.

The implications of these for the curriculum are considerable. The curriculum permeates all aspects of classroom life, since every decision a teacher makes in the classroom is directly or indirectly concerned with promoting learning by establishing and maintaining an environment which caters for the wide range of ability and temperament represented in any class of children.

Thus, 'commonsense' or implicit theories are instrumental in informing teachers' decision-making. What makes this possible is the autonomy of the primary teacher in his or her own classroom. In this most important and most elusive factor, the personal and the professional in teaching are intimately bound up and are only in general terms reducible to something called teaching style.

The way in which primary teachers' classroom autonomy originated and developed has shaped teachers' attitudes to curricular and organizational change. Primary education has its origins in the elementary school system established in the mid nineteenth century to provide a complete and cheap as possible education for working-class children. Dearden (1968) has considered its social utility curriculum:

Principally, of course, this meant the teaching of the three R's: reading, writing and arithmetic. It was thought useful that these children should be able to read, be able to write neatly, legibly and with correct spelling and punctuation, and be quick and accurate in the main departments of the social applications of arithmetic such as number, money, weight, length, capacity and time. In addition to these 'basic skills', a certain amount of factual material came also to be included, so that something of the geography of the British Isles and the British Empire was learned, a suitably patriotic view of our national history was formed, and some facts about certain biological phenomena were learned. Very important also was a knowledge of the Bible. *(p. 3)*

Teachers made few if any decisions about the curriculum since what was taught in the early years of elementary education was virtually determined by the Revised Code, whereby children were tested each year on the three R's by the inspectorate and were promoted or remained in the same standard according to their tested attainment. The teacher's salary was determined by the results he or she gained. This system of direct accountability and curriculum control was not abolished until the 1890s by which time the characteristic authoritarian ethos, mass instruction methods and narrow curriculum were established in elementary schools, despite attempts by the Board of Education to widen the curriculum and liberalize teachers' views of schooling from the early twentieth century onwards.

The transition from elementary, as being a complete system, to primary, as being the first of a number of stages in education, was slow, hindered in part by the retention of the elementary system long after the idea of stages in educational provision had been officially accepted. The growth of secondary education confirmed even more the inferiority of elementary schooling. Teachers in its early years were poorly educated, over-trained, had few promotion prospects except within the system, and had a low social status compared with teachers in other types of school. Yet the system succeeded within its own narrow terms of reference.

But it is something of an oversimplification to say that the elementary system was the direct precursor of the primary school since the aims and ethos of the two are so different. Elementary education

was conceived of as being an education complete in itself, fulfilling
particular instructional, social and moral goals; primary education
was seen as the first of a number of stages in an educational process
through which children were initiated into the skills, values and
knowledge appropriate to the beginnings of education. The stages
were conceived of as interdependent and equal in status. While it
can be claimed that nursery and infant schools and departments
developed early on a recognizable ethos of child-centredness, junior
schools and departments tended towards a greater formality of
method and attitude reminiscent of the elementary ethos. In
Blyth's (1965) terms, the preparatory rather than the developmental
tradition was more influential in shaping practice in junior schools.
Yet there were strong official pressures towards liberality evidenced
by the 1904 Elementary Code, the 1905 Handbook of Suggestions
to Teachers, the Hadow Reports of 1926, 1931 and 1933 and the
Butler Education Act of 1944. The Hadow Reports especially took
note of research into the nature of intelligence and aspects of
development and how these might be reflected in schools. It is hard
to say how directly influential any of these pronouncements were in
actually bringing about shifts in attitudes resulting in change in
schools. Because of the world depression in the 1930s, education
was heavily under-financed in Britain at a time when many
innovatory ideas were developing. At one point teacher education
programmes were curtailed and teachers' salaries cut by ten per
cent. This central government intervention as a result of long-term
economic troubles coupled by a fall in the birthrate throughout the
1930s slowed educational growth both in terms of provision and
development.

It was not until the 1950s that educational thinking and research
acquired a social dimension. The notion that social-class membership and family background are major factors in the development of
educability pervades the Plowden Report of 1967 and is as strong as
its child-centredness. The tensions between what were understood
as social influences and the trend towards making the individual
child the focal point of the educational process placed teachers in a
difficult position. On the one hand, the family was claimed to be a
stronger influence than the school in promoting educability and on
the other, 'starting with the child' in terms of working from

children's needs and interests and respecting individual differences among children required teachers to believe that every child had the potential to learn in the school setting. It is a tension that is by no means resolved today after the experimentation in the 1960s and 1970s with programmes of 'compensatory' education in inner-city areas following Plowden's positive discrimination recommendations, the emphasis on group and individual learning and the trend away from streaming by ability.

How teachers respond, in the context of their autonomy, to what they perceive to be the main influences and constraints which combine to structure the situations in which they work, will indicate how they see themselves as teachers, and where the limits and possibilities of their autonomy lie. A study which threw considerable light on this considered teachers' perceptions of the physical, ideological and personal factors in their schools and classrooms which appeared to constrain and influence their management of the curriculum (Taylor, Reid, Holley and Exon, 1974). It involved one hundred and twenty teachers in twelve schools chosen as being representative of good primary education by the local authority inspectorates. Teachers were surveyed about their attitudes to teaching roles, curriculum change and educational aims. The study focused on the conditions influencing practice and how these related to teachers' views on the aims of primary education. Influences and constraints were identified; through these, researchers were able to focus on the interrelationship between the intended and the operational curriculum and consequently on teachers' classroom decision-making. What emerged is that, while teachers felt that they exercised freedom in their own classrooms, they had little influence over policy-making in their schools. Classrooms and schools were perceived as two separate areas of activity which had the effect of safeguarding teachers' classroom autonomy. In functioning within these two areas, aims were of little importance to teachers; there was little agreement on what was important and teachers did not attach much significance to formulating aims or in reappraising what they took to be functioning aims. As Boydell (1978) comments: 'Given the magnitude and complexity of the issues at stake, it is perhaps hardly surprising that teachers seemed to balk at the notion of reflecting on aims.' (p. 43-4)

What kind of professional autonomy is this? What emerges is a picture of primary teachers maintaining their professional self-esteem and equilibrium through exercising responsibility in their own classrooms but placing a low value on reflecting on their own activities apart from expressing a general approval of child-centered methods. Part of the survey concerned the kinds of influences which could be reciprocated by teachers. There was a considerable variation in what teachers felt they could reciprocate, but agreement on there being a low level of general reciprocity. There is not so much an equilibrium between classroom autonomy and participation in school decision-making, but rather that acceptance of the first entails a rejection of the second. If such decision-making was participated in, Taylor *et al.* argue, then teacher's classroom autonomy in the traditional English sense would be diminished but their level of professionality raised. As a consequence, teachers would become more open to appraisals of their activities. In Hoyle's terms, restricted professionality, which describes a somewhat insular type of competence in the classroom setting, would give way to extended professionality, in which classroom competence is tempered by the teacher's awareness of a wide social and ideological frame of reference.

It is consistent with these factors that the teachers surveyed inclined towards a child-centred view of primary education of which a basic premise is that teachers' first responsibility is towards the children in their classrooms and the fostering of close teacher–pupil relationships so that the curriculum can be based on the understanding of children's needs and interests. Teaching methods and classroom organization are the major concerns especially where children's learning is organized in small groups or individually. What may be described as the curriculum is conceived of in terms of individual and small group work and only as a tentative ground-plan for the whole class. Since child-centred teachers, according to Taylor *et al.*, do not have a global view of the curriculum, they are likely to have limited horizons so far as change is concerned:

Of course the arguments in this chapter stem from a presumption that change is needed in the primary school curriculum and in the ordering of its aims. This may not be the case. But if it were, the barriers to innovation might prove formidable not only because in general teachers are neutral to change but also because they are not able to visualise a range of alternative possibilities. This lack of vision, if it is such, may be reinforced by the teacher's preoccupation, and success, with the children he teaches. *(Taylor et al. 1974, p. 62)*

This might be seen as an over-critical or negative opinion of child-centred teachers but it helps to make an important point about what teachers who accept this view of learning and teaching consider to be their most important concerns. It emerges also in such recent research into classroom processes as the Leicester University-based ORACLE work. In summary, there is a strong concern for pedagogy, that is, the methods, procedures and resourcing of teaching and learning, and less concern for content especially in the form of organized schemes. This attitude can be traced back to the reaction by child-centred learning advocates against the strictures of the elementary schools, expressed as antipathy for a laid-down curriculum which indicated to them a character-moulding or a filling-up-of-empty-vessels mentality applied to children's learning.

The very nature of child-centredness, the placing of that abstraction, 'the child', at the focal point of the learning process, stresses the need to identify his educational requirements and to take these as the basis for arranging learning experiences. The classical account of child-centredness suggests that since these at best can be anticipated, rather than identified, through a prearranged classroom environment, the main job of the teacher is to provide a variety of possible curricular resources from which the child will choose according to the dictates of his interests. This, of course, is an extreme picture, to the point of caricature. The reality is that teachers are more likely to provide for certain learning activities through the materials and equipment that they make available and that children will be guided towards suitable choices. But the basic transaction is the same, whatever the degree of child-centredness, and it works against the idea of planning the curriculum as a whole and in advance. Curriculum concerns will be focused on better ways of resourcing learning, such as providing more effective concrete apparatus, work-cards and sheets and investigation materials.

But the school and societal contexts of autonomy are changing. There is a growing self-evaluation movement which is part of the trend for local authorities, spurred by the DES, to require schools to adopt a more consciously planned approach towards teaching and learning. The negative aspects of the context is continuing financial stringency, a falling primary school population since the mid 1970s but expected to rise in the mid 1980s, the practice of shedding teachers 'surplus to requirements' through early retirement, and considerable unemployment among newly qualified teachers. The last of these is ominous; never before has the teaching force been better educated and qualified, with a rapidly growing number of graduates in primary and secondary schools.

Although school-based development and school-focused in-service training is increasing, there is a more pervasive and perhaps more authoritative influence arising from pressures towards commonality in the curriculum, originating from the DES and Her Majesty's Inspectorate and expressed in a number of policy and discussion papers published since 1977. These can be interpreted as attempts to systematize patterns of learning which traditionally have been decided by teachers in their own classrooms, especially in primary schools. Closely related to this movement is the growing requirement for teachers to be able to account for their practices. The terms of reference of the DES's Assessment of Performance Unit are the monitoring of children's attainment across the curriculum. There is the potential, given the political climate, for the results of monitoring to be used as norms of attainment which teachers would be expected to achieve. The movement from a descriptive, research operation to a prescriptive, politically motivated one which is concerned with achieving teacher efficiency through teachers' attainment of learning which can be tested and measured has been discussed in detail by Lawton (1980) and in Lacey and Lawton (eds.) (1981). This is not to claim that the conditions which have produced the technician teacher in some states of the USA have been brought about in Britain. Rather, there are underlying conflicts, not yet very powerful, between the increased under-standing of the nature of teaching and learning and of the ideological contexts in which education is practised which many experienced teachers have acquired through in-service study, and what they see as limitations on their professional activities. The most direct of these is limited prospects as the cuts take effect. More pervasive is the question as to whether the self-evaluation and accountability movement reduces teachers' roles to that of technicians or whether it leads to enhanced professionality. Head teachers in primary schools, in most local authorities, increasingly are in the position of being required to monitor learning but there is little agreement on the most effective and suitable ways of doing this.

Thus, issues to do with accountability, self-assessment and curriculum change have become part of what it is to be a teacher in the 1980s rather than being marginally relevant features of school and classroom life which can be avoided if they threaten classroom autonomy. Indeed, the concept of autonomy itself is changing as teachers become more and more involved in curriculum planning which applies to the whole school.

1. Theoretical foundations of the primary curriculum

Nature and aims of education

It is a truism to claim that educational processes are intentional by nature since they are designed to achieve some goal or end-product that would not be achieved through the random acquisition of skills or understanding. The idea of a planned learning experience usually but not necessarily involving teachers and learners working towards a common goal is the main characteristic of an educational process. Skills are learned so that they may be applied and knowledge must be of something. While there are no disputes about the goal-directedness of education, disagreement is possible about the nature of the end-results that might be aimed at and achieved through it. Disputes about aims highlight differences between views of education which by their very nature are not reconcilable; it is through statements of aims that distinctive views of the nature of education can be discerned. For example, those who see education as being essentially liberal, aimed at developing cognitive perspective and the 'educated man', maintain that education is worthwhile in itself. They would deny that it can be harnessed to produce responsible members of society or economically viable individuals because this would devalue education by ascribing to it aims which are extrinsic to the educational process. In this view, education can have no aims other than more education: the educated person is in practice unachievable because it would be impossible to decide on, let alone apply, criteria to find out whether someone was fully educated or not. So, education is reduced to a form of socialization, or schooling, if goals to do with social action or economic viability are the end-results aimed at. By making the learner an instrument, the possibility of self-development, self-realization or personal autonomy is denied. Historically, the 'schooling' viewpoint is neatly encapsulated in the description of a satisfactory elementary school education in the Newcastle Report of 1861, while the Clarendon Report a few years later gives an account of an adequate classical liberal education for young gentlemen which has everything to do with cultivation and self-enlightenment.

There are echoes of this fundamental difference of viewpoint in the continuing 'product v. process' arguments about models of curriculum design and planning. These two extremes focus on the status of the learner and the nature of learning and at the level of philosophical discourse help one to decide whether an experience is educational or not. For example, it would be odd to describe as educational situations where limited skills were inculcated by being drilled into pupils so that they reproduced the skills without needing to think about them. But if there is the intention to apply these to higher order or compound skills, then this will be brought about through developing understanding of something larger than just those skills, and the process could be defined, again on philosophical grounds, as being educational. The main point is that there are distinguishing conditions which when applied to a teaching–learning situation will help someone to decide whether it is educational or not, and that all these processes have some sort of end-result in mind.

Debates about the merits and deficiencies of different models of curriculum design are tantamount to debates about different views of education. Through them, different assumptions are made about the position of the learner in relation to the teacher and different conceptions of school knowledge arrived at. For example, it might be thought that a view of planning which maintained the importance of using objectives would project an instrumental view of education in which there were certain finite goals to be achieved in the long term such as inducting individuals into the value system of their society. Or, a view which stresses processes and principles of procedure rather than end-results might indicate a view of education in terms of self-development and the intrinsic worth of knowledge. Advocates of both would need to come to terms with the practicalities of learning and teaching: could education be practised if there were no rewards or punishments, no requirements for compulsory attendance or no legitimated authority for teachers to order and organize classrooms? Discussions and disputes over different views of planning are pointless if they do not acknowledge this practical context with its constraints and possibilities. Notions about planning educational experience are not motivated by a desire to theorize for its own sake but are attempts to provide a framework or structure in which the elusive nature of the educational process can be made more controllable and predictable. This applies to all views and models of planning, from those which take prespecified behavioural objectives as their focus of attention, to those which repudiate objectives and consider processes in learning and teaching to be central to planning.

Characteristically, models of planning tend to originate from some perceived deficiency in an education system which the model seeks to correct. Thus, the American educator, Ralph Tyler, who has been influential in developing models which take objectives as their starting point, was concerned in the 1930s with the over-emphasis in American education on psychometric approaches to testing attainment and the curricular narrowness both in content and methods that this engendered. In trying to establish a framework which would help to liberalize curriculum theory and practice, he posed four questions:

1   What educational purposes should the school seek to maintain?
2   What educational experiences can be provided that are likely to attain these purposes?
3   How can these educational purposes be effectively organised?
4   How can we determine whether these purposes are being achieved?

These denote four aspects or dimensions of curriculum planning which have become imbedded in all subsequent debates about its nature. They are objectives, content or knowledge, its organization for teaching and learning, and evaluation and assessment. Together they make up a simple linear model, with the first task of the teacher being to decide on and specify objectives, then to choose suitable content to achieve these, to arrange this in appropriate learning experiences, and finally to assess children's work in order to evaluate whether or not the laid-down objectives have been achieved. Because of its simplicity such a model can be used to plan the day-to-day work in a classroom or it can be applied to long-term schemes. Tyler's attempt to systematize purpose and direction in education was not new since educators such as Bobbitt in the 1920s and earlier had also thought in terms of setting objectives in order to apply scientific rigour to the processes of teaching and learning.

Curriculum planning by objectives

What informed these early attempts to organize curriculum planning around objectives was the desire to be able to state in advance what pupils would achieve in their learning through experiencing a lesson or a scheme, with such learning being seen as desired changes in pupils' behaviour. Through learning something people literally are changed and such changes should be discernible to teachers. A hierarchy of behavioural changes could be brought about in pupils which would be in keeping with the broad social and personal aims which a society would expect its education system to accomplish. This idea of controlled and monitored educational planning is present in varying degrees of development and explication in all state-maintained education systems and can be discerned in legislation and official reports on different aspects of the systems. It is at its most clear when the guiding principles are spelt out, if only at the slogan level. In American thought and practice a view of equality is sustained in which similarities rather than differences in

objectives ⟶ content ⟶ learning experiences ⟶ evaluation

Figure 1   *Tyler: rational curriculum planning*

people are important and in which environment predominates over genetic inheritance. Education is the means by which individuals will be inducted into the norms and values of a complex, changing multicultural society. This was so at the beginning of American mass education in the nineteenth century and applies to the highly complex and socially mobile population of today. Educational planning is also the means by which teachers can be made more efficient and cost-effective, a factor which was as important a hundred years ago as it is today.

From the 1920s onwards a range of influences and circumstances in America combined to give prominence to planning by objectives, a movement which reached its most developed form in the 1960s. Among these was the overriding belief that by using them teachers would become more effective in bringing about learning; the development of a positivistic psychological view of learning which stressed measurable outcomes; the underlying pragmatist philosophy influencing American educational thought and practice which laid particular emphasis on the identification and use of ideas that generate practice that can be publicly evaluated; and the position of a mass education system, committed to the educating of a melting-pot school population, which took guidance of the individual in accordance with the values of an emerging democracy as its main task. Such trends can also be seen in child development studies, particularly in Gesell's work. What became known as rational curriculum planning was summed up by its main advocate, Ralph Tyler (1949):

Many educational programs do not have clearly defined purposes. In some cases, one may ask a teacher of science, of English, of social studies, or some other subject what objectives are being aimed at and get no satisfactory reply. The teacher may say in effect that he aims to develop a well-educated person and that he is teaching English or social studies or some other subject because it is essential to a well-rounded education. No doubt some excellent educational work is being done by artistic teachers who do not have a clear conception of goals but do have an intuitive sense of what is good teaching, what materials are significant, what topics are worth dealing with and how to present material and develop topics effectively with students. Nevertheless, if an education program is to be planned and if efforts for continued improvement are to be made, it is very necessary to have some conception of the goals that are being aimed at. These educational objectives become the criteria by which materials are selected, content is outlined, instructional procedures are developed and tests and examinations are prepared. *(p. 3)*

The effect of such concentration on one model of curriculum planning was to elevate it to the status of definitive model for American educators. In Britain, objectives-based planning only began to be discussed in the mid 1960s with the early large-scale curriculum development projects mounted by the Nuffield Foundation. The reaction to it was instinctive distrust, and it was seen as an American over-intellectualizing of essentially practical matters, as evidenced by Maclure (1968a) in his report on the Third International Curriculum Conference held the previous year. This gut reaction from all strata of the teaching profession confirmed that working from objectives was not accepted as the definitive basis for planning. The mood was, and perhaps still is, anti-planning. There are several reasons for this, many of which were discussed in the Introduction. First, there is the distrust of systematizing or indeed of theory applied to practice. Second, there is the considerable classroom autonomy of teachers in Britain contrasted with their relative lack of influence over school policy-making. Such a position is likely to engender a sense of self-sufficiency so far as their own teaching is concerned. Third, there is the tendency for teachers in Britain to reject the idea of there being educational experts in the form of curriculum developers, but to accept higher-level practitioners such as subject consultants, advisory teachers and inspectors so long as they can be identified as practitioners. In other countries, including the USA, expertise in specific roles such as curriculum developer, evaluator, or researcher is recognized. Fourth, there is the child-centered stance of primary education in Britain which is anti-planning in spirit even though it is by no means the way in which all primary schools operate.

The development of primary education in Britain needs to be seen in terms of the spirit of child-centredness rather than its practice: Bennett's study of teaching styles and the more recent ORACLE work draws attention to the diversity of styles in operation and to the degree of teacher autonomy they point to. Of all the factors mentioned, autonomy is the most crucial for curriculum planning. What it usually implies in terms of planning is that teachers typically select the curriculum range for their children, perhaps on a termly basis, with actual schemes of work hardly ever being in a written-down form. The main organizational mechanism is likely to be records of individual children's progress, especially in language and mathematics, to provide a basis for advancing their learning by given them more difficult tasks. In general, the younger the children the more detailed the individual records will be. With older juniors there is likely to be a wider curriculum coverage but the extent of record keeping for individual children is likely to be less detailed. If the school curriculum operates with guidelines and syllabuses these will be reflected in each teacher's plans according to his or her opinion of their suitability and quality. Since primary teachers have the generalist function of being responsible for the whole curriculum, in contrast to the secondary teacher's single subject specialist function, teachers in primary schools have almost total control over their children's curricular experiences. It is not a situation which lends itself to systems of curricular organization, and least of all to one which is as tightly structured as an objectives-based scheme. But many teachers acknowledge the need for a structure which is more than simply implicit in their teaching, and this is particularly so when they have been involved in curriculum innovation. A good example of this is the experience of the developers of the Schools Council Science 5–13 Project which is the only large-scale attempt to innovate in primary education which used an objectives approach. Again, the experience of the developers with a previous, less structured project, the Nuffield Junior Science Project, prompted them towards more structure.

Science 5–13: an objectives-based project

This is the only major project in this country to use behavioural objectives. It began after the Nuffield Junior Science Project ended in 1966. The earlier project adopted a discovery learning approach in which teachers in the trial schools developed their science teaching in collaboration with the project team. These trial schools were asked to develop science work on a discovery learning basis, to report their experiences and to use a wide range of equipment. The intention was to publish these case studies of success and difficulties in order to reach teachers beyond the trial schools. Two Teachers' Guides were published, setting out the project's rationale and including a number of case studies of good practice, together with two other source books and some background readers. But the project did not 'take' for a number of reasons. The discovery approach which entailed starting from children's environments and the scientific questions they raised about these was not accepted by all teachers. Many also lacked the confidence to teach science because of the paucity of their own scientific knowledge. The project team arguably did not give enough direct help because it was over-concerned about the dangers of being diverted from its rationale and producing teacher-proof kits, though there was no pressure on it to do this. The project ended before the team had been able to solve these problems, as Wastnedge (1972), the director, recalls:

The hundreds of teachers and thousands of children were left on their own. What no one perhaps appreciated was that this kind of impetus could soon be lost, once the teachers involved were deprived of practical help and support in their classrooms during the difficult early days. The teachers who were with us in the pre-trial days always had team members on hand ready to help and advise. As a result they produced some astounding work. But after that the teachers had too few supporters – and then none at all. The project ended. *(P. 39-40)*

It was however developed in a highly structured form in primary schools in Ontario following visits to the trial schools in Britain by science teaching inspectors.

The Science 5–13 Project began nine months later with a new team using many of the earlier trial schools. It sought to develop a resource-based scheme through source books related to discovery approaches but with a large number of hierarchically arranged objectives providing a detailed structure. These objectives existed in draft form but several of the trial-school teachers saw them and wanted to use them. Reluctantly, the team allowed this and was thereby committed to an objectives approach. The teachers' guide, *With Objectives in Mind* (1972), mirrors this cautiousness:

> It is true, as we have pointed out, that there are certain dangers about having objectives that are closely specified; they may, for instance be so detailed or so inflexible that they leave no elbow room for either teacher or child ... Thus a position of some delicacy has to be established. The objectives, whatever they are, must not intervene between teacher and pupil; they must be present in the teacher's mind, but not so far in the forefront of it that she sees them rather than the children and the ways in which she can meet their needs. *(p. 7)*

This sums up well the British primary teacher's attitude to objectives. The project has not succeeded in establishing primary science in the schools ten years after it ended and after three supplementary projects aimed at increasing teachers' knowledge and skills for teaching science. There is some suggestion that teachers like and use the resource books but ignore the teachers' guide, the objectives being thought to be too complicated or irrelevant. Also there is the inherent tension in the design, brought about by trying to reconcile a discovery learning pedagogy with a behavioural objectives plan.

Objectives: possibilities and problems

How readily applicable or otherwise are objectives? Popham (1969) is in no doubt of their necessity because of their effectiveness:

> We are at the brink of a new era regarding the explication of instructional goals, an era which promises to yield fantastic improvements in the quality of instruction. One can only sympathise with the thousands of learners who had to obtain an education from an instructional system built on a muddle-minded conception of educational goals. *(p. 33)*

But this was written in the USA in the late 1960s when rational curriculum planning was at its most influential and persuasive. It was the basis for a large range of curriculum development projects, especially those having to do with the development of compensatory education programmes. Educationalists such as Mager (1962; 1975) were less concerned with the need to argue the cause and more intent on the mechanics of writing behavioural objectives. Because of the need to specify objectives in advance, as argued by Tyler for instance, the notion that objectives are of necessity behavioural came to be widely accepted. But it needs to be made clear that educational objectives span a continuum from the tightly framed behavioural such as 'By the end of this lesson all the children in the group will be able to count accurately from one to ten' to the more general objectives, which strictly speaking are not behavioural, which are to be found in the Science 5–13 teachers' guide: 'Ability to classify living things and non-living things in different ways' or 'Recognition of the role of chance in making measurements and experiments'. Even more general are those objectives which denote conceptual understanding such as 'Formation of a broad idea of variation in living things' and those which have an affective bias such as 'Enjoyment in exploring the variety of living things in the environment'. Some objectives therefore are close to being broad aims. The only thing that these different kinds of objectives have in common is that implicit in their wording is the requirement that they state what the learner will or should achieve in learning.

What might be the practical advantages and disadvantages in working with objectives? Eisner (1969) in his discussion of instructional and expressive objectives claims that behavioural objectives have four limitations. First, there is the assumption that through them all educational outcomes can be predicted; second, that widely differing subject matter is treated as if it were the same in terms of the degree of specificity possible when designing objectives; third, that they tend to confuse the application of a standard and the making of a judgement in assessment; and fourth, that there is the implication that forming objectives is the first task when planning curricula and that this confuses the logical with the psychological in planning. There is also the problem for Eisner in that establishing a direction and formulating an objective seems to be seen as one and the same thing. He also raises the potential problem of objectives causing a reduction in the range and depth of teaching and learning, since a strict interpretation of a behavioural objectives planning

approach would insist that only what overtly can be measured can
be planned. There are two aspects here. First, primary teachers
have oversight of the whole curriculum and formulating objectives
for this coverage would result in an impossibly large number.
Eisner estimated that an American elementary school teacher
would need to formulate 4200 objectives in a single school year in
order to organize all that he or she was teaching. The second aspect
has been mentioned earlier: if only what is visibly assessable is to be
included as valid potential learning experiences for children, then
this would have the effect of reducing the sum total of legitimate
learning to that which is measurable. What it indicates is that
affective factors such as attitudes, points of view, emotions and
expression would have to be left out, but Popham and others
disagree with this. According to Popham it is both possible and
desirable to apply objectives to the expressive arts. He suggests an
example: 'Having been given a previously unencountered literary
selection from nineteenth-century English literature, the student
will be able to write the name of the author and at least three valid
reasons for making that selection.'

What this leaves out in the study of literature is fairly obvious.
Where does reasoned appreciation and enjoyment come in, how is
quality expressed? The effect is to reduce literature to the level of
quiz-show-type questions. The point in planning by objectives
surely is to achieve the objective through studying the content and
this is feasible if the objective is appropriate and does justice to the
content. It should not be a matter of deciding on the objective and
then choosing material in order for learners to achieve it, which is
Eisner's point about planners confusing the logical with the
psychological in planning.

In the same discussion, Popham vigorously defends behavioural
objectives mainly by setting up a number of possible objections and
refuting these. Some of these raise genuine problems which
continue to reverberate beyond Popham's refutations and rejoinders.
They include, for instance, charges of triviality being attributed to
an objectives approach, the way in which objectives prevent
teachers from taking advantage of the unexpected in learning, the
possible dehumanizing effect of working from objectives, that
teachers do not as a matter of course plan in this way, and that

curriculum activities such as the fine arts and the humanities cannot be planned in this way. Popham's reply to the last two is that teachers should be induced to plan in this way, and that while it is difficult to write objectives for the fine arts and humanities, teachers should persevere. He offers the example of judges in diving contests being able to give fine gradings which generally agree. If they can do it, surely teachers can identify criteria for expressive arts activities and use them as a basis for formulating objectives?

Eisner also raises the question of whether this is a natural way for teachers to plan:

> Why is it that teachers do not eagerly use tools that would make their lives easier? Perhaps because they are ignorant of how objectives should be specified . . . perhaps. But why should those who know how objectives are to be specified disregard them in their own course work? Perhaps because they have acquired 'bad' professional habits . . . perhaps. Is it possible that the power and utility assigned to objectives in theoretical treatises are somewhat exaggerated when tested in the context of the classroom? *(Eisner 1969, p. 3)*

His argument for distinguishing between what he terms instructional and expressive objectives is important more because of the stand it takes against the all-pervading nature of behavioural objectives than for its power to convince. He takes instructional objectives to be much the same as Tyler's, Popham's and Mager's behavioural objectives:

> Instructional objectives are objectives which specify unambiguously the particular behaviour (skill, item of knowledge, and so forth) the student is to acquire after having completed one or more learning activities. *(Eisner 1969, pp. 14-15)*

That is, they are suitable instruments for the teaching and assessment of such short-term learning as simple skills which may be applied to more complex learning tasks. Expressive objectives are descriptions of what Eisner terms an educational encounter:

> It identifies a situation in which children are to work, a problem with which they are to cope, a task in which they are to engage; but it does not specify what from that encounter, situation, problem, or task they are to learn.

An expressive objective provides both the teacher and the student with an
invitation to explore, defer or focus on issues that are of peculiar interest or
import to the inquirer. An expressive objective is evocative rather than
prescriptive. *(Eisner 1969, pp. 15-16)*

His examples of expressive objectives include: to interpret the
meaning of *Paradise Lost*. To develop a three-dimensional form
through the use of wire and wood. To visit the zoo and discuss what
is of interest there. These sound more like general principles of
procedure than objectives, and Stenhouse (1975) queries whether
they can be counted as objectives because of their open-endedness.
They sound more like learning tasks which children will engage in
than the results of learning as befits objectives. But this raises the
question of how specific in practice can workable objectives be. For
example, the objectives, claimed to be behavioural in the Science
5–13 Project are much more general as statements of intended
learning than extreme advocates of behavioural objectives planning
such as Mager and perhaps Popham would allow. But the team was
aware of the danger, in their opinion, of objectives getting in the way
of discovery learning and thereby interposing between teachers and
their children.

There could also be technical problems in trying to achieve
specificity in framing objectives, according to MacDonald-Ross
(1973), which are due to ambiguities in the functions of verbs in the
English language. The general rule for objectives writers is to stick
to verbs of action (to develop; to use) and to avoid verbs of state (to
know; to understand) but English verbs do not divide neatly into
these categories. He cites research which demonstrates how
difficult it is for people to decide whether a verb describes an
observable behaviour or not. Part of the problem lies in the
direction taken by what he calls the 'hardliners', whose understanding
of the use of objectives originated from strategies designed to train
personnel to use complicated machinery during the Second World
War. The man–machines training systems worked well for these
highly structured but essentially simple training situations but it is
a further question as to whether they will carry over successfully to
the different context of the school and classroom. The 'softliners',
among whom he includes Tyler and Popham, are well aware of the
need to root objectives in educational situations and of the

problems in writing them which this causes.
that the instrumental view of education
adopting a similarly instrumental view of
could the task of producing objectives be fac
indoctrination, and in the reduction of e
mentioned earlier. It leads him to suggest that the concept of an
instructional objective is easy enough to grasp, but that an
educational objective is virtually a contradiction in terms.

For primary teachers, objectives-based planning appears to have
serious limitations because of the child-centredness which is at the
heart of English primary education, at the level of ideology if not
fully realized in practice. Some learning such as early reading and
computation lends itself to an objectives approach and indeed so do
reading materials of the programmed workshop type as well as
mathematics schemes which are designed as a linked series of
observable learning points. By contrast, the subject-centredness of
much secondary education seems to lend itself more readily to an
objectives approach except that the content emphasis itself provides
an adequate framework without using objectives.

Most of this chapter so far has been a discussion of the nature,
applicability and limitations of planning by objectives with the
emphasis being placed on specific or behavioural objectives. This is
in accord with the dominance of the viewpoint and its continued
influence, not in curriculum development, but in the range of self
and institutional evaluation strategies that are being developed in
answer to the challenge that teachers ought to be accountable
publicly for their professional activity. Performance and management objectives have become recognized instruments for assessing
and evaluating schools and teachers; they are also as controversial
and as mistrusted as their earlier manifestation as curriculum
planning objectives.

Process approaches to curriculum planning

If planning by objectives is in conflict with the child-centred ethos
of primary education then an emphasis on the processes of teaching
and learning rather than the learning products might be more

appropriate to the experiential nature of much primary practice. This of course assumes that explicit planning of any kind would be accepted by teachers. There is a sense in which planning according to processes is more a reaction against planning by objectives than a model of planning in its own right. Probably the best expressions of processes are to be seen in curriculum development and in accounts of classroom practices. While there is an established literature on planning by objectives, this is not the case with processes. Stenhouse (1975) makes this point when discussing curriculum evaluation based on objectives; the evaluation accounts read as if they are aimed at an academic audience rather than teachers. Stenhouse is a forceful critic of objectives and as director of the Humanities Curriculum Project he was able to express and develop a major innovation based on a processes view of planning. He maintains that education consists of four processes: training, instruction, initiation and induction. Objectives are suitable in the case of training since performance through the exhibition of skills is central to it. Instruction also implies directed learning of the kind which is appropriate for objectives setting. He is particularly concerned with induction which he sees as the main business of education:

Education enhances the freedom of man by inducting him into the knowledge of his culture as a thinking system. The most important characteristic of the knowledge mode is that one can think with it. This is in the nature of knowledge – as distinct from information — that it is a structure to sustain creative thought and provide frameworks for judgement. *Education as induction into knowledge is successful to the extent that it makes the behavioural outcomes of students unpredictable.* (Stenhouse 1975, p. 82)

Objectives then by definition do not meet the knowledge requirements of learners for this to be achieved. He maintains that the forms of knowledge which are the basis for the school curriculum make it possible for teachers to select content for a curricular scheme without recourse to objectives because the form itself is a structure which embodies procedures and concepts:

For the key procedures, concepts and criteria in any subject — *cause, form, experiment, tragedy* — are, and are important precisely because they are, problematic within the subject. They are the focus of speculation, not the object of mastery. Educationally, they are also important because they invite understanding at a variety of levels. The infant class considering the origins of a playground fight and the historian considering the origins of the First World War are essentially engaged in the same sort of task. *(Stenhouse 1975, p. 85)*

This notion of a spiral of concepts and ideas moving from the simple and specific to the complex and generalizable but retaining the same identity is important to the process view of planning. It is in accord with guided discovery and project approaches in primary schools, where the conclusion is not simply where the child ends up but is implicit in the child's investigations. It would be to distort learning to assign objectives to this, the point being that it is of the nature of an inquiry that directions change through problems being solved. There is rarely a final conclusion; in Pring's words, 'What is important to achieve is broad agreement on principles of procedure rather than objectives to be attained.'

There remain questions as to how general an application Stenhouse's approach might offer from its origins in the humanities. Also, is his view of objectives too specific? Whitfield (1980) claims that behavioural objectives serve to indicate the kinds of behaviour which characterize the end-results of learning rather than prescribing specific end-results. The distinction is important since if this is so the nature of 'behavioural' can be more broadly defined than Stenhouse and others such as Pring (1973), and Sockett (1973) would allow. Whitfield also claims that Stenhouse has taken the classical usage, of prespecifying what pupils will learn, as definitive, which is a misunderstanding of the terminology.

The belief that the consideration of processes in learning and teaching should be at the heart of curriculum planning is also expressed in Bruner's idea of a spiral curriculum, whereby learners visit and revisit the basic principles which form the structure of a body of knowledge. His views are presented in the powerful claim that 'Any idea or problem or body of knowledge can be presented in a form simple enough so that any particular learner can understand it in a recognisable form.' (Bruner 1968, p. 44) He maintains that people have three ways of knowing which are also modes of representing understanding: the enactive, which is through action, the iconic, which depends on visual and other sensory information, and the symbolic, which is essentially linguistic. These superficially resemble Piaget's stages in concept acquisition but Bruner sees them as emphases in development which will be utilized according to the demands a particular learning problem makes on the learner.

The structure of any body of knowledge can be presented in three different ways which accord with these modes: by a set of actions, or a set of images or by symbolic or logical propositions. He gives the example of a balance beam to illustrate how these work. A young child can act on the beam as he would on a see-saw and by doing so can demonstrate for himself how the beam works. In this way he comes to an understanding of the principles governing its operation. An older child can represent it by a model or a drawing, while finally the beam can be represented by language or by mathematical equations referring to Newton's Law of Moments.

For Bruner, as for Stenhouse, planning has everything to do with identifying the principles which form the structure of a body of knowledge, and then organizing the learning experiences which will enable learners to get on the inside of that discipline or subject. The learning process is cyclical rather than cumulative and individual to the learner; it is therefore by its nature unpredictable. Bruner draws most of his examples from mathematics and the physical sciences but his most developed expression of planning as process is his Man a Course of Study (MaCOS) project, a social science programme for 10 to 12 year olds in American elementary schools but modifiable for older children. It relies on imaginative and complex resourcing through films, slides, tapes, books and exercises; the teacher's role is to arrange this rich learning environment in such a way that children come to address the central questions — what is human about human beings? How did they get that way? How can they be made more so? – with increasing insight and sophistication. MaCOS is evolutionary in that it makes problematic the distinctiveness of humankind and its potential for development. Though the learning style is highly structured, considerable teacher and learner choice is possible in the arrangement of the units making up the project and the amount of time spent on each.

Stenhouse and Bruner come nearest to systematizing process; whether their attempts constitute models is a further question.

Certainly they both accord with the deeper notion of education as being a process which has been imbedded in the concept of education and of what it means to be educated from Plato onwards, compared with working with objectives, which represents a counter-claim in the interests of efficiency, predictable learning outcomes and direct teacher accountability. There is also the claim that planning according to processes is closer to the realities of learning and teaching; significantly, Bruner and Stenhouse each realized their views through the highly practical means of curriculum development projects which were both innovatory and widely accepted by teachers.

Planning in practice

Curriculum planning from the viewpoint of theoretical underpinnings and conflicting ideologies has been treated at some length here. But how do teachers see planning? Eisner has expressed his doubts about the practicability of planning by behavioural objectives and the study carried out by Taylor (1970) suggests that he is right so far as teachers in Britain are concerned. Eisner made the point that the requirement to start with objectives resulted from a confusion between the logical and the psychological in planning. This too is borne out in Taylor's research:

To some extent, the way in which teachers think about curriculum planning is an inversion of how the theorists think about it. For the theorist, curriculum planning usually starts by stating aims and objectives, the purposes the curriculum is to serve, and this is followed by a description of the learning experiences necessary to achieve the aims and objectives. These learning experiences are the context which the teacher must attempt to create for his work, together with some indication of how pupils may be interested and involved in learning . . . .

Teachers, on the other hand, appear to start, understandably enough, with the context of teaching, follow this with a condsideration of the kind of learning situation likely to interest and involve their pupils and only after this consider the purposes which their teaching is to serve. Lastly and as an issue of lesser importance, teachers consider criteria and procedures for evaluating the effectiveness of their course of teaching. *(pp. 59-60)*

What is clear from this research and the forgoing arguments here is that teachers do not see that any one theory or model of planning necessarily fits their practice. They are unconvinced of the effectiveness of objectives and in some ways disturbed by their implications, and they hold commonsense or implicit theories about planning which are both specific enough to inform day-to-day classroom activities and general enough to count as views about the nature of education. Hargreaves (1979) has argued that such implicit theorizing which informs teachers' practice but which rarely breaks surface is the key to understanding why teachers function in the way they do, and to those values in which they believe which give authority to their planning.

For this reason it is important to try to make explicit what usually remains implicit. Teachers do not as a matter of course articulate their values or seek to justify their practices because for them, theory and practice are interdependent. When they are asked to do this they often find it difficult, as if the interrelationship was beyond words, for example, in the case of 'Mrs Carpenter' in Sharp and Green's study of ideologies in conflict in a council estate primary school. Skilbeck (1972) has also approached this issue in considering strategies for curriculum change. He is especially concerned with processes of change in schools. Since curriculum planning is an aspect of curriculum development, his arguments have a bearing on the possible applications of planning models.

He suggests that there are three basic models of development: the rational deductive, the rational interactive and the intuitive. The first takes effect in centrally controlled education systems in which policy and the means by which it is implemented is determined centrally. The schools' role is simply to put policies to work with teachers being little more than skilled technicians. In the rational interactive model, decisions are shared between local government officials, teachers and possibly parents and children. A wide range of interested parties contribute to the implementation of broad policies which are interpreted according to local needs. Teachers' professionality is invoked in their roles as course developers, evaluators and examiners. The notion of teacher as curriculum researcher which Stenhouse has developed is implicit in this model. In the intuitive decision-making model, the individual classroom becomes the focal point, with teachers acting in accordance with their understanding of their pupils' needs at the time. This becomes their only role, with understanding, integrity and vitality being the looked-for teacher qualities.

Skilbeck suggests that the rational interactive model has the most potential and he proposes how it might be implemented and developed. A key feature is the situational analysis: through carrying out an analysis of their own teaching situations, and arguably they are the only ones in a position to do this, teachers will be able to decide the direction of possible change and to plan its implementation. Although the analysis assumes the use of objectives, these do not form part of a tight, closed structure as in rational curriculum planning.

Reid (1981) in a more consciously theoretical paper considers a number of perspectives on the curriculum which underpin different approaches to planning and development. He calls these: the systemic, the radical, the existentialist and the deliberative. He is most concerned with the last of these, through which, he argues, teachers are best able to consider issues of fact and of value in curriculum decision-making.

To be deliberate is to show a concern that is broad and careful. Deliberative theory is evolutionary in its social philosophy and pragmatic in its

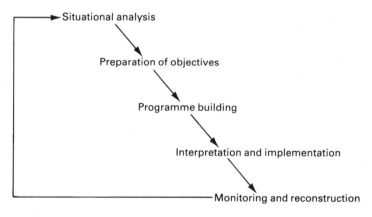

Figure 2 *Skilbeck's situational analysis*

conception of how knowledge should relate to policy and action. But it has carefully articulated value commitments and a distinctive method. *(p. 168)*

While the other perspectives are systems-bound, the deliberative is eclectic:

The role of the theorist is to help individuals and institutions to find the resolution that fits their case. It will be unique. Not universal, nor one of a standard set. And though what is decided will represent, ideally, a consensus it need not be a crude compromise. Deliberation can be inventive. It does not endorse the managerial view that the model for the resolution of competing views must be based on the 'zero-sum' game. *(Reid 1981, p. 176)*

So the need is for eclecticism since no single model is likely to match the complexities involved in any one planning situation. For primary teachers, this is compounded by their generalist role in relation to the curriculum. Normally they teach everything to all their children and there will be a tight connection between their individual teaching styles, how they organize their classes and how they perceive the task of planning. It might be appropriate to think in terms of objectives when planning basic language work or number operations, for example, but even here it is difficult to think only in terms of objectives. There is a concern for the kinds of learning processes set up when children are investigating the properties of numbers and developing a sight vocabulary. What is important is to bring into focus particular concepts which are likely to provide the basis for solving practical problems; the idea of a planning continuum as illustrated below will be helpful in that it encourages an eclectic view. By this is meant that specific planning endeavours, whether they are single lessons which deal with skills, or longer-terms classroom projects such as a local study, or whole school schemes for a curriculum area such as language or science will need to draw on aspects of curriculum design as these are applicable to the lessons, projects or schemes.

Questions about planning raise practical questions about how best should teachers assess and evaluate learning. The present concern for teachers' accountability and the development of

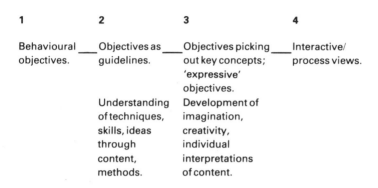

1	2	3	4
Behavioural objectives.	Objectives as guidelines.	Objectives picking out key concepts; 'expressive' objectives.	Interactive/ process views.
	Understanding of techniques, skills, ideas through content, methods.	Development of imagination, creativity, individual interpretations of content.	

Figure 3   *Curriculum planning: a suggested continuum*

methods for institutional and self-evaluation are in danger of producing a kind of lowest common denominator check-list mentality in local authorities which are considering the performance objectives schemes developed in parts of the USA. These make the assumption that teachers also plan strictly by objectives. Accompanying this belief is the view that if all classroom learning is visible, it will be easy to record. Such views illustrate the way in which learning and teaching can be artificially reduced to what is measurable in education in the interests of accountability. The thinking has everything to do with Popham's reply to the charge that as planning in this way is not a true reflection of teaching, teachers do not as a matter of course use objectives. His response was unequivocal: they should be made to use them.

Evaluation

Much can be implied so far about the nature and practices of evaluation from the discussion of curriculum planning. Simply, those who advocate working from objectives, and especially behavioural objectives, take an assessment view of evaluation in which the single most important piece of information about a project or a scheme or a lesson is the learners' measurable performance. By finding out what has been learned in terms of the laid-down objectives, it can be decided how far these have been achieved. But there are different accounts according to whether objectives are conceived as being behavioural or simply specific. For example, Tyler, the leading 'soft-liner' says:

The process of evaluation is essentially the process of determining to what extent the educational objectives are actually being realised by the program of curriculum and instruction. However, since educational objectives are essentially changes in human beings, that is, the objectives aimed at are to produce certain desirable changes in the behavior patterns of the student, then evaluation is the process for determining the degree to which these changes in behavior are actually taking place. *(Tyler 1949, pp. 105-6)*

In contrast, Mager (1962), a leading 'hard-liner' says:

Here is an example of a more appropriately stated objective:

When the learner completes the program of instruction, he must be able to identify by name each of the controls located on the front of the Target Tracking Console.

What words tell what the learner will be doing demonstrating the achievement of the objective? The words 'identify by name'. The objective communicates to the learner the kind of response that will be expected of him when his mastery of the objective is tested. *(pp. 13-14)*

As this approach developed, various alternative and modifying views of evaluation became prominent. The worthwhileness of a learning process, not necessarily demonstrated through evaluating its objectives, was suggested as being as valuable as finding out what the learners had learned. Scriven (1967) made an important distinction between evaluation which is formative, that is, where there is an on-going evaluation strategy which provides information about the programme which can be used to effect changes in it en route, and summative evaluation which takes place after the programme is ended and which is likely to focus on what demonstrably was learned from it. Summative evaluation characterizes objectives-based schemes. Its weakness on its own is that the scheme is completed before its effectiveness or otherwise can be established: as Bruner says, it is like doing military intelligence after the war is over.

There has been a shift towards considering the processes operating within programmes and to place more emphasis on these than on what was visibly learned. By studying how the programme was perceived by learners and teachers, how choices of activity or materials were made, how much interest and enjoyment there was, it is claimed that more fundamental and useful evaluation information will be obtained than by collecting test scores and records of attainment. It marks a shift away from a psychometric measurement of learning orthodoxy towards an approach in which the worth-whileness of the experience itself is under scrutiny. Parsons (1976) traces the relationship of this development to the anthropological styles of classroom research which were displacing the measurement-orientated approaches in the early 1970s. In his words, the concern is not only with 'How good is it?' but also with 'What is happening?'

This 'illuminative' approach, pioneered in Britain by Parlett and Hamilton (1972) depends on participant and non-participant observation, interviews and questionnaires centred on the processes of learning:

The aims of illuminative evaluation are to study the innovatory programme: how it operates; how it is influenced by the various school situations in which it is applied; what those directly concerned regard as its advantages and disadvantages; and how students' intellectual tasks and academic experiences are most affected. It aims to discover and document what it is like to be participating in the scheme, whether as teacher or pupil; and in addition, to discern and discuss the innovation's most significant features, recurring concomitants and critical processes. *(p. 10)*

Opponents of this approach argue that it is too subjective and too dependent on the evaluator's sympathies and not enough on his expertise in observing and analysing. Some attempts at illuminative-style evaluation have been overtly hostile to measuring learning performance; in Parlett and Hamilton's view, this represents 'agricultural-botanical' evaluating where learners are treated as if they were plants in an agricultural testing station.

Also, there are growing critiques from people who have been involved in curriculum development and who are suspicious of ideological standpoints in evaluation which might work against trying to find out what was good or bad about an innovation. The trend is towards an eclectic style of evaluation in which methods are adopted because of what they can contribute in particular evaluation situations, as Williams (1981) points out:

In practice though, it does mean that we cannot rely on a single source or type of data. An evaluation will need to draw on as wide a range of evidence as possible including test scores, teachers' and pupils' opinions, observations and so on. This will permit the evaluator to draw conclusions which rest upon a number of different kinds of data giving a better based conclusion, a process usually referred to as triangulation by analogy with the trigonametrical process. In educational research Occam's Razor may be more powerful than the most sophisticated analyses. *(p. 84)*

This in turn raises a number of questions about the role of

'Objective' ——————————————————————————— 'Subjective'

1 'agricultural botanical type.	2	3	4	5 'illuminative' type
Behavioural objectives. (Mager)	Less strictly behavioural. (Tyler)	General objectives for key concepts.	Goal-free. (Scriven) Portrayal (Stake)	Detailed picture of scheme built up through observation, organization, interpretation of data.
Quantitative style of evaluation.				Qualitative style of evaluation.
Measurement of attainment at end of lesson or scheme.	Measurement of attainment throughout lesson or scheme.	Measurement of attainment and concern for process throughout lesson or scheme.	Balance between attainment and process.	Attainment less important than question of worthwhileness. Process in a scheme or lesson emphasized.

Figure 4   *Curriculum evaluation: a suggested continuum*

evaluator. As Lawton (1980) has pointed out, evaluation is not a neutral activity; evaluators will devise schemes which are in agreement with their own value positions regarding educational change. This of course is easily detectable when evaluators are operating at either point on the evaluation continuum as 'measurers' or 'illuminators'. (Figure 4)

An eclectic approach, then, entails that evaluation methods are designed with particular evaluation tasks in mind: Steadman's (1981) approach is characteristic:

> From one point of view evaluation provides evidence for decision-makers: i.e. for the teacher attempting something new, for colleagues whose co-operation is required, or for the head-teacher or local education adviser from whom further resources are required. Thus an evaluation technique should provide information which is valid, reliable, relevant to the concerns of the decision-makers, and available in time to help the decisions. *(p. 211)*

His is essentially a technical approach aimed at those teachers who are likely to be involved in evaluation in their own schools. He considers techniques under five headings: formal feed-back, measurement of attainment, assessment of attitudes, description of the curriculum context, and processes and analysis of curriculum materials. The discussion is very much from the point of view of what teachers might select as methods in terms of these five in order to carry out a comprehensive and bias-free evaluation.

The checklist to be used as a basis for planning an evaluation compiled by Harlen and Elliott (1982) again stresses eclecticism. They suggest five questions which should guide any evaluations: what are its purposes? What information is required to serve these purposes? What methods can be used to gather the information? How should the information be reported? How should the report be used to achieve the original purposes? The ten factors they list which need to be taken account of when planning deal with value questions such as worthwhileness as well as methodology; they also raise questions as to who will have access to the evaluation information. Again, the approach is aimed at the production of full and unbiased evaluations which can be used as bases for decision-making in a school.

Curriculum knowledge

Much has been written about the nature of curriculum knowledge over the past twenty years with the major philosophical perspective being argued by Hirst (1965; 1970; 1974) in Britain and Phenix (1964) in the USA. It is important to survey the main line of argument at this point because of its implications for the different forms a common curriculum might take; this will be considered in Chapter 7.

Broadly, the mainstream argument is in favour of disciplines, or forms of knowledge, in Hirst's terms, as providing the most secure basis for curriculum planning. Hirst, in discussing the limitations of school subjects compared with forms of knowledge, suggests that they have arbitrary qualities which have largely been brought about by accidents of history. These include their utility, their characteristic assessment by examination, and the relative status of subjects within a school curriculum.

Much of this suggests a closed system resisting change. It might be asserted that school subjects, whether primary or secondary, are in some sense logically constructed: they are an attempt to identify content which has common features but as soon as the emphasis is placed on content, many divisions between subjects begin to look arbitrary and the subjects themselves take on arbitrary characteristics. This is best demonstrated by the long-standing influence of examinations on what is taught, certainly in secondary schools and projected down to some extent to junior schools. If outside influences such as examination boards and employers succeed in bringing about changes in the range, status and content of subjects in a curriculum, then it can be argued that the subjects themselves no longer represent internally consistent patternings of knowledge which are inherently worth studying, but become means to ends.

The question could also be raised as to whether school subjects can be seen otherwise than instrumentally since they have been conceived of in many different contexts other than the strictly educational. These include vocational training, being the precursors of and the means by which people attain the right to higher academic study, and the means by which pupils can be classified in a school through right of access to subjects. There is also the relative status of subjects, the main criterion being their different academic qualities with the 'practical' subjects like home economics and craft and design technology being inferior to 'theoretical' subjects like mathematics, history and the physical sciences. When Hirst and Peters (1970) claim that school subjects have no ultimate value outside a school context their arbitrary quality and means–ends status are underlined.

Hirst's account of forms of knowledge is an attempt to define the basis of curriculum planning by establishing seven forms which are equal in educational value and logically consistent. They are: formal logic and mathematics, the physical sciences, 'awareness and understanding of our own and other peoples' minds', moral judgement and awareness, aesthetic experience, religion and philosophy. He maintains that they have four main features which establishes their autonomy as forms of knowledge or disciplines. These are: central concepts peculiar to particular forms, a distinctive logical structure made up of interconnecting concepts, distinctive expressions or statements, and distinctive methods of establishing the truth or validity of propositions which each generates. From these seven can be derived an infinite number of fields of knowledge which can be theoretical or practical, such as geography and engineering, for curriculum planning purposes. Hirst's conviction is that these seven are necessary for the development of rational autonomy, and he takes the main objective of education to be the development of mind. It follows that these form the basis for a common educational experience for all children since they all share the same aims and are equally valuable.

There are a number of objections and problems. A major one has to do with the number and differentiation of the forms themselves. Are the forms as complete a demarcation of human understanding as Hirst claims? Has the attempt to establish a certain number of specific forms resulted in an artificial reduction in the number of conceptual structures which constitute knowledge? Another concerns the logical structure of Hirst's disciplines with systems of interlocking concepts forming a hierarchy in a form of knowledge, with concept A being logically prior to concept B and so on. This might be relatively easy to chart in mathematics, for instance, and to a lesser degree in the physical sciences. It seems to become increasingly difficult to establish such priority in religion, morals, aesthetic activities and the human sciences. These are basic questions which can be applied to any disciplines-based account of knowledge such as Hirst's or Lawton's (1969; 1973; 1975; or Dearden's (1968).

Such questions are important in curriculum planning since what is planned is likely to be a compromise between what seems to be required on the grounds of the promotion of rationality or autonomy – the values position – and what is historically and socially determined – the status quo position. There is an inevitable tension between aims which stress individual autonomy and those which emphasize social participation and personal economic viability as discussed earlier here. But commitment to some form of commonality which has a rational basis and is not simply a reflection of teachers' implicit understanding of what should be included in a curriculum, or an attempt to refine the present curriculum is beginning to develop. What might be termed the 'administrators', the DES policy-formers and Her Majesty's Inspectorate, have produced several papers in the period 1977-81 and though most of these emphasize secondary schooling, a considered view of education between 5 and 16 years is beginning to evolve. The 'educators' – theorists such as Hirst, Lawton, White and Dearden – have influenced this system-building through the frameworks and points of reference they have presented. Dearden's work in primary education is unique and therefore especially important; it, together with the issue of curriculum commonality with its connected implications, for common content and common standards, will be examined in Chapter 7.

Summary

It is the intentional nature of educational processes which distinguish them from other kinds of situation where learning may take place. This is not disputed; rather, there are disputes over the aims of education between those for instance, who see it as intrinsically worthwhile and others who attribute social and instructional goals to it. Such disputes are implicitly about the nature of education itself. They have a parallel in 'product v. process' arguments in curriculum design where, on the one hand there are advocates for prespecified learning as a result of an educational process, and on the other, where the process itself is valued. The rational model of curriculum planning developed by Tyler in the USA in the 1930s takes the setting of objectives as its main feature. This notion of planning became the dominant one for curriculum planning in the USA and has had a pervasive influence in debates on planning in Britain since the 1960s. The Schools Council Science 5–13 Project was however, the only large-scale attempt to use behavioural objectives. What it in fact demonstrated was the inherent tension between child-centred teaching and learning approaches and the attempted prespecification of learning.

The range of different types of objectives needs to be acknowledged, with the possibilities and problems they offer to teachers in their curriculum planning. But it also needs to be recognized that there are serious difficulties in working with objectives, beginning with the sheer technical difficulty of accurately formulating them. A process approach to planning respects the interaction between teachers and learners which is characteristic of experiential learning but in no developed sense is it a model of planning. It is partly a reaction against the artificiality of predicting what children shall learn and the reductionism which results, and partly an affirmation of the deeper notion, of education being a process. The practical answer is eclecticism in planning, where specific solutions are designed for specific planning tasks.

Views about the nature and practice of evaluation closely conform to these two opposed positions, from the contention that evaluation constitutes the measurement of children's attainment to the notion of evaluation being the illumination and portrayal of processes. The most recent development is towards eclecticism where a range of methods combine to form an evaluation strategy designed to fulfil a specific task. This is very much in accord with the growth of school-based curriculum development.

So far as the nature of curriculum knowledge is concerned, the mainstream argument is broadly in favour of disciplines. Hirst criticizes the arbitrary qualities of school subjects and takes the main aim of education to be the induction of people into disciplines, or forms of knowledge, which he maintains constitute the basis of any rationally ordered school curriculum. This approach has been developed more with the secondary school in mind but Dearden has developed a primary curriculum based on a Hirstian forms of knowledge approach. Since each discipline is of equal value, together they imply curricular commonality, a concept which is being developed with some degree of agreement between the 'administrators' and the 'educators'.

Further reading

Hamilton, D. *et al.* (eds.) (1977), *Beyond the Numbers Game*, London: Macmillan
  A reader in evaluation theory and practice which covers a wide range of approaches.
Stenhouse, L. (1975), *An Introduction to Curriculum Research and Development*, London: Heinemann.
  Chapters 5–7 are a critique of objectives and the development of a process view of planning.
Tyler, R. (1949), *Basic Principles of Curriculum and Instruction*, Chicago: University of Chicago Press
  A clear exposition of the nature and use of objectives in planning by an influential figure.

2. Primary school ideologies and curriculum planning

Child-centred education

The dominant ideology of primary education is clearly that of child-centredness. The arguments for child-centredness grew partly out of a profound dissatisfaction on the part of humanist educationalists with the rigidity and authoritarianism of the elementary school system, and partly as a result of a new, liberal view of children's learning. Children were seen as taking an active rather than a passive role in their own learning in response to their inner drive towards individual growth and development. By implication, in the child-centred view, teachers were seen less as instructors and moulders of character and more as organizers of learning environments to facilitate individual children's growth. For the first time in education, childhood was seen as being valuable in itself and to be respected as a stage in human growth. Growth was a natural process and the teacher's task was to stimulate it according to its implicit laws.

The rationale for child-centredness was to be found in psychological research and thinking which emphasized the nature of individual differences; the work of Freud and especially that of Piaget were important. Likewise were philosophical positions such as Rousseau's which extolled the naturalness of childhood and its vulnerability in the world of adults. Materialist theories of knowledge such as those of the empiricist philosophers Locke and Berkeley were instrumental in providing justification for children's explorations of their environments through play and discovery learning since sense impressions of the physical world were held to be the means by which knowledge was acquired.

The curriculum planning implications are broadly that it is wrong to impose curriculum content on children; indeed, the whole notion of there being 'a curriculum' which is derived from the culture of a society and which embodies knowledge and skills into which children will be inducted is alien to child-centredness. So too is curriculum planning, by deciding in advance for a group of children which skills they will master and which concepts they will learn.

While the Hadow Report of 1931 is cited as being the first developed official statement on child-centredness in primary education, the notion is there in such early pronouncements as the 1904 Elementary Code and the 1905 Handbook of Suggestions to Teachers:

The teacher must know the children and must sympathise with them, for it is of the essence of teaching that the mind of the teacher should touch the mind of the pupil. He will seek at each stage to adjust his mind to theirs, to draw upon their experience as a supplement to his own, and so take them as it were into partnership for the acquisition of knowledge. *(Maclure, 1968b, p. 160)*

Within this statement are the main lines of development which reached their fullest articulation in the Plowden Report of 1967. These include the assertion of the need to place the child at the centre of educational experience, the notion of the teacher as enabler of learning, with the linked notion of the child being the agent of his own learning, and the need to take account of children's personal and individual development in the learning situation. The key figures in this basic rationale for primary education were Dewey and Piaget in this century, with Froebel and Rousseau as background figures in an earlier period. About Dewey, Curtis and Boultwood (1965) say of his early life, that it produced:

two outstanding convictions which directed the whole course of his educational work — a conviction that traditional methods of schooling were futile and fruitless, and an even firmer conviction that the human contacts of everyday life provided unlimited natural, dynamic 'learning situations'. *(p. 463)*

He was very much in the American nineteenth-century pragmatic tradition in that he tested and developed his educational views in the practical climate of a laboratory school he established at the University of Chicago where he was head of the Department of Philosophy and subsequently Director of the School of Education. The experimental school did not use extreme approaches, but with experienced elementary teachers working with small groups of children, kept to the curriculum and methods of public elementary schools. Teachers were alerted to the possibilities of curriculum integration, especially in basic skills learning, and to the use of different materials and equipment. They were also concerned with activities that merged school and community life since it was Dewey's belief that:

The fundamental factors in the educative process are an immature, undeveloped being; and certain social aims, meanings, values incarnate in the matured experience of the adult. The educative process is the due interaction of these forces. Such a conception of each in relation to the other as facilitates completest and freest interaction is the essence of educational theory. *(Goldby, Greenwald, West (eds.) 1975, p. 150)*

Growth is the central concept, the 'primary fact with which education deals' and he sees it as being developed in the context of the group and the community rather than as individual self-realization in the Froebellian sense. If education is not merely a preparation for life but life itself, for children, then schools must involve children in learning experiences which link the school with the outside community. In simple societies, the family provides these experiences but complex industrial societies with formal education systems need, themselves, to be educative. If the school initiates the young into an educative society, then dualisms such as distinguishing between play and work, and conflicts between formal and informal approaches in education will cease to be important. So far as curriculum planning from this standpoint is concerned, the idea of a subjects-based curriculum is rejected as being alien to the way children perceive the world. It might be justifiable logically but not psychologically:

Again the child's life is an integral, a total one. He passes quickly and readily from one topic to another, as from one spot to another, but is not conscious of transition or break. There is no conscious isolation, hardly conscious distinction. The things that occupy him are held together by the unity of the personal and social interests which his life carries along . . . .

Again, in school each of these subjects is classified. Facts are torn away from their original place in experience and rearranged with reference to some general principle. Classification is not a matter of child experience; things do not come to the individual pigeon-holed. *(Golby* et al. *(eds.)* *1975, p. 151)*

He talks about the fundamental opposition of child and curriculum when curricula are organized into subjects. This can be overcome if teachers perceive children's interests, attitudes and activities strongly enough for them to develop curricula which take account of these. But this is not a matter of slavishly following children's interests; what children exhibit as potential growth points must be interpreted and appraised in terms of those learning activities which will be in a child's interest to pursue. There is a danger too of treating a child's interests as being important in themselves. Dewey does not declare what the framework might be for appraising interests, only that teachers should sponsor those which are central to a child's well-being and capable of development. He therefore places considerable emphasis on the professional understanding, skills and responsibilities of teachers at a time when formal methods, a subjects-based curriculum and mass instruction were the norms in elementary schools both here and in the USA, and teachers' status depended more on their ability to control and coerce than to facilitate learning.

He suggests that there are three difficulties when this child-curriculum polarity dominates. First, there is no organic connection between the children's experiences and experiences represented in text books and teaching materials, so such material will be rendered inert. Second, the textbook material is not related to any problems or issues in the children's lives and it therefore lacks motivational potential. Learning through it will be mechanical and lifeless.

Third, it is impossible for materials to be so ordered that they match the thought processes of individual children; all they can do is to assume a generality of such processes which are then imposed on children in the teaching situation. Such material thus becomes a substitute for thinking rather than a promoter of thought. He further suggests that there are problems in that children can become accustomed to tasks which are mechanical and routine to the extent that they come to enjoy them. This has the effect of stultifying learning by preventing children from developing their own interests. Also it is possible to make such materials presentable by imposing penalties such as punishment or ridicule if it is not learnt. Through this 'psychologizing' of teaching content the raw material for learning can be made palatable to children. Dewey reiterates that this is not to assert that children's concerns deny the possibility of content but that content cannot be preordained:

Action is response; it is adaptation, adjustment. There is no such thing as sheer self-activity possible – because all activity takes place in a medium, in a situation, and with reference to its conditions. But, again, no such thing as imposition of truth from without, as insertion of truth from without, is possible. All depends upon the activity which the mind itself undergoes in responding to what is presented from without. *(Golby* et al *(eds.) 1975, p. 163)*

Dewey's most visible influence can be seen in the development of what were called 'activity' methods in progressive primary schools, both fee paying and state, provided in the 1930s. How closely these adhered to his strictures depended on how much of his philosophy was understood or accepted by advocates. At worst, children's interests were accepted uncritically as the recognized basis for developing their learning: teachers saw their roles as organizers of environments which children explored on their own terms. The result often was much time-wasting, tension between children and teachers, and frustration on the part of parents. At best, children contributed to the learning environment through close interaction with their teachers who perceived critically their interests and translated these into learning needs by establishing a learning milieu which emphasized guided interest and choice. Dewey therefore was important in laying the foundations for a liberal interactive model of primary teaching in which the acquisition of basic skills as tools used to explore child environments were valued rather than being seen as valuable in and for themselves. Certainly, in the hands of skilled and knowledgeable teachers, topics, projects and centres of interest became effective means by which children were educated.

If Dewey provided the rationale and framework, it was the work of Piaget, as adopted by child-centred theorists, which most clearly informed the methodology of experiential learning. While Dewey's influence has been pervasive, Piaget's has been direct and practical, which is ironic considering that while Dewey was profoundly concerned with education and its development, Piaget was uninvolved with schools and had conservative views about the nature and aims of education. Through Piaget it was possible to argue for the individuality of children to be accepted as the main basis for planning learning, for defending the worth of discovery methods and of the value of play for young children. The role of the teacher in organizing learning environments and the principles of curriculum integration were also consolidated in primary schools through Piaget. His research became important to child-centred exponents at a time when scientific justification for their views was being asked for in the form of research into children's development which could be applied to teaching methods. If Froebel was an important figure in establishing the ethos of child-centredness and Dewey had pointed out the way it must be developed in terms of the child and his relation to the curriculum, Piaget was especially influential in providing the rationale for teaching approaches. Experiential learning is necessarily the underlying ideology of child-centredness since the distinction between pupil and teacher is blurred, with the child not only becoming the prime agent of his own learning but also being authoritative about his educational needs.

In this interactive teaching–learning climate teachers have the responsibility for identifying children's readiness for learning. Piagetian thinking was at the heart of the Nuffield Primary Mathematics and Junior Science Projects, and the Science 5–13 Project took Piaget's sequence of stages of concept acquisition as the means by which the range of objectives could be located according to the demands they made on children at different stages of cognitive development. The Plowden Committee, too, acknowledged his influence:

Although he is not primarily an educationalist, his work has important implications for teachers. His observations of the sequence in the development of children's concepts are being tested on samples of children in many countries and these tests are tending to confirm his main findings. Much more investigation is needed on the extent to which the school environment and the guidance and teaching provided by teachers can accelerate children's progress. The effect of social expectations on the way children learn also calls for study. Nevertheless Piaget's explanations appear to most educationalists in this country to fit the observed facts of children's learning more satisfactorily than any other. It is in accord with previous research by genetic psychologists and with what is generally regarded as the most effective primary school practice, as it has been worked out empirically. *(Para. 522, pp. 192-3)*

It is not proposed to go into detail here about Piaget's stages of concept acquisition. In summary they are as follows:

1   Sensori–motor (0-2 years). The beginning and development of motor and mental skills; establishment of a self-identity; learning through exploration and play.
2   Pre-conceptual (2–4 years). Play is still important; imitation of adults and older children; learning by linking events in a cause–effect sequence.
3   Intuitive (4–7 years). The child is dependent on superficial perceptions of his environment and forms ideas about it impressionistically. Does not have the maturity to test his concepts against evidence other than what he sees and experiences himself.
4   Concrete operations (7–11 years). An operation is defined as an internalized act. The child's reasoning is almost exclusively tied to concrete events. His thinking is patterned by what he directly perceives and he does not fully understand such concepts as conservation of number, area or weight.
5   Formal operations (11–adolescence). This will be reached at different times for different concepts. Those to do with weight and number are likely to be achieved first, then volume and density. Abstractions such as justice

and fairness will come later still. What characterizes formal operations is the ability to reason hypothetically in the absence of material evidence.

The processes which make concept acquisition possible are assimilation, when people absorb and organize experiences around the activities that produce these, and accommodation, where new situations experienced resist the activity patterns people subject them to, to the extent that they develop new patterns.

There have been a number of critics both of Piaget and of attempts to co-opt his research findings in support of educational practices. The key issues so far as the second of these is concerned are children's so-called needs and interests in an educational setting, readiness for learning, and discovery learning approaches. They all have a direct bearing on curriculum planning both in the classroom and in the form of large-scale projects. Bruner (1968), whose work has partly been a development of aspects of Piaget's thought, suggests what Piaget's real task was, in contrast to how he has been interpreted by educationalists:

Unquestionably, the most impressive figure in the field of cognitive development today is Jean Piaget. We and the generations that follow us will be grateful for his pioneering work. Piaget, however, is often interpreted in the wrong way by those who think that his principle mission is psychological. It is not. It is epistemological. He is deeply concerned with the nature of knowledge per se, knowledge as it exists at different points in the development of the child. He is considerably less interested in the processes that make growth possible . . . Rather it is his brilliant formal description of the nature of the knowledge that children exhibit at each stage of development . . . What he has done is to write the implicit logical theory on which the child proceeds in dealing with the intellectual world. (pp. 6-7)

If this is so, it makes for considerable problems in that the co-option of research findings and conclusions from one frame of reference does not as a matter of course hold true in another context. Piaget's epistemological findings do not necessarily hold up without distortion in an educational setting: there is the fundamental logical problem of proceeding from a statement of fact to a statement of value. To develop this: Piaget stresses the importance of children investigating their environments in order to develop their conceptual understanding; educationalists stress the importance of discovery methods in schools in order for children to learn effectively in school. Piaget's statement is descriptive, originating from his research; the educationalists are stating what ought to be the case in co-opting an aspect of Piaget's work to support a policy of teaching and learning. He did not, for instance, produce a theory of learning, as Bruner points out, yet many educationalists have treated his work as if it contained such a theory. An example of this is the mystification which attaches to the notion of learning readiness. Piaget, in identifying a number of stages which form a logical sequence in which children move from very concrete conceptual understanding to more abstract understanding, made it clear that development is uneven, that there is a danger in ascribing precise ages to stages, and that individuals will move through the stages at a pace dictated by their individuality. When this is placed in a classroom context there appears the problem of identifying which stage children are in, or where they are in a particular stage, and how far that stage has been consolidated in the range of activities that make up a primary school curriculum. Children on this account will be ready to move on to the next stage once they have consolidated the present one in the activity, be it mathematics or language, or art and craft. Piaget stresses that children learn through interacting with their environments, and this justifies on the face of it an activities-based discovery approach founded on children's demonstrable learning needs. One of the means by which teachers discern needs is through the interests children display. Needs therefore can be conflated with interests and taken as a sign of a child's growing maturity. But how reliable a guide is this for planning in the classroom? Dearden (1968) suggests:

When we are presented with views about 'readiness' then, it is worth asking at least these four questions: (i) Readiness for what exactly? (ii) Are the conditions for readiness necessary, as are physiological and conceptual conditions, or only in your view desirable? (iii) In either case, can these conditions themselves be actively brought about, or must we wait for some inner ripening to take place according to 'the laws of growth'? (iv) If the conditions are not necessary but only in your view desirable, what are the values by which your views on desirability can be taken to be warranted and how do you justify them? *(pp. 31-2)*

In an NFER survey on teaching of reading practices in 100 infant schools and departments, documented by Goodacre (1967), 48.5 per cent of the teachers took attitudes to reading activities such as interest shown in all kinds of books and interest shown in the printed word generally, to be the main determinant of reading readiness, that is, a child would be considered ready to be taught to read if some of these were observed. Perceptual abilities which have to do with physical maturation were recognized as a determinant by just under 20 per cent of the teachers. The Plowden Committee acknowledged that readiness was important for teachers to discern but noted that 'It has sometimes been thought of in too negative a way.' Bruner is in no doubt about its status:

The 'curriculum revolution' has made it plain even after only a decade that the idea of 'readiness' is a mischievous half-truth. It is a half-truth largely because it turns out that one *teaches* readiness or provides opportunities for its nurture, one does not simply wait for it. Readiness, in these terms, consists of mastery of those simple skills that permit one to reach higher skills. *(Bruner 1968, p. 29)*

Dearden, similarly, has raised questions about the interpretation of children's needs and interests and the notion of growth that underpins child-centred approaches.

While experiential learning characterizes child-centredness, the views on which it is premised can be challenged because of the mixture of co-opted research evidence, philosophizing, and the ordinary reaction against more restricted and authoritarian teaching which inform these. But in spite of counter claims, child-centredness remains the dominant ideology of primary education. As argued before, this not to say that the majority of teachers accept it to the extent that they put into it into practice. While the fact of individual differences and the educational implications which this raises has been accepted in a general way, the pedagogy for effectively catering for difference has yet to be developed. The University of Leicester based ORACLE research project into primary classroom processes and their implications for teachers has established four basic styles of teaching. What the researchers describe as the 'individual monitors' was the most prevalent with 22.4 per cent of the teachers observed coming into this category. Galton, Simon and Croll (1980) described these teachers as follows:

The general impression gained from a variety of accounts provided by observers is of pupils working mainly on individual tasks with teachers under a considerable amount of pressure. They move rapidly from table to table but sometimes sit at their desks with pupils queuing up either for information or clarification of the instructions in the text book or work sheet . . . .

Within such a complex organisation the task of monitoring the pupils' work takes a high priority. It is important not only to correct books but also to record progress so that where pupils are involved in planning their own timetables regular checks can be carried out to see if each pupil has fulfilled his quota. *(p. 122)*

These teachers are responding to the requirement that individual children need individual attention, but the heavy reliance on graded worksheets, assignment cards and structured texts has the effect of distancing children from the teacher. Children proceed at their own pace in teachers' eyes but the pace is dictated by the grading of their work. Such distancing is caused by the virtual impossibility of individualizing children's learning for a class of thirty or so with the usual ability range to be found in unstreamed classes in infant and junior schools. The effect is mechanistic and 'instructional' in the pejorative sense, yet it is a response in good faith to the plea to treat children as individuals. The researchers' 'group instructors' teaching style comprised 12.1 per cent of the sample and these more closely approached the Plowden model of the teacher:

Set against the general low level of cognitive questioning these teachers do nevertheless engage in above-average amounts of open questioning. This suggests that they allow the groups of pupils to offer alternative answers to problems and do not always insist on theirs being the one correct answer. Such teachers appear to come closer in adopting the grouping strategy suggested by Plowden for coping with large-sized classes. *(Galton et al. 1980, p. 123)*

The Plowden Report

The report was seen as the apotheosis of child-centredness and
sixteen years after its publication many of the questions it raised are
still issues. Among these are the roles of teachers in guiding
experiential learning. The arguments are somewhat tentative since
the emphasis earlier in the report on the need to recognize
individual differences strongly suggests that the class-teacher
organization which remains the norm in Britain lends itself
too readily to whole class teaching. So while the committee is in
favour of the class-teacher system since it underpins teacher's
classroom autonomy and offers stability, it also argues the need for the
class to be broken down into smaller teaching units. It agrees that
individualized work has increased but it points out the danger of
over-individualizing the curriculum to the detriment of maintaining
a high level of interaction between teachers and children. So group work
is seen as the most positive compromise and there is the suggestion that
teachers might ability-group their classes for basic skills learning.
The committee was, however, against streaming by ability as a
method of organizing schools. What, then, is argued for is a balance
of whole class, group and individual work, on the grounds that this
is manageable, and that the breadth of the curriculum can be
covered in this mixed form of organization. There is some
suggestion that older children might benefit from a team-teaching
organization where teachers function according to their particular
curriculum strengths and interests. Galton, Simon and Croll claim
that the report does make other more general points about
organization which have to do with teacher's responsibilities for the
curriculum, the physical layout of classrooms and resources and
teaching aids.

So, the committee takes a conventional view of classroom
organization, one that has not markedly changed in the sixteen
years since the report appeared. The short section on the teacher's
role says little about this except that it is broad and ill-defined. The
plea is made for the identification of individual differences and the
satisfaction of consequent learning needs. This raises questions
about adequate curriculum coverage:

Similarly, as we have surveyed the way children learn, the demands made on teachers have appeared frighteningly high . . . . Far more knowledge, both about subject matter and about how children learn, is called for in teachers, who have continually to exercise judgement, to 'think on their feet', to keep in mind long-term and short-term objectives. *(Para. 875, p. 311)*

Since the report dwells on how children learn, much in consequence is said about teaching approaches. This compares with the fairly slight treatment of classroom organization and the teacher's role.

As might be expected, the committee's treatment of the curriculum is very much in terms of its views on learning. There are certain problems to do with methodology and the organization of content which lie at the heart of child-centred education and which are encapsulated in the report. The committee's views on the curriculum are summarized in the first paragraph in Chapter 17, Aspects of the Curriculum:

Throughout our discussion of the curriculum, and particularly in this and the previous chapter, we stress that children's learning does not fit into subject categories. The younger the children, the more undifferentiated their curriculum will be. As children come towards the top of the junior school, and we anticipate they will be there till 12, the conventional subjects become more relevant; some children can then profit from a direct approach to the structure of a subject. Even so, subjects will merge and overlap and it is easy for this to happen when one teacher is in charge of the class for most of the time. *(Para. 555, p. 203)*

The committee then proceeds to discuss the curriculum in terms of separate subjects. The curriculum, then, initially is conceived of as being undifferentiated to fit the view of the child as school learner which the committee proposes, and then it is discussed as being made up of Religious Education, English, including speech, reading, poetry, drama and writing, Modern Languages, History, Geography, Mathematics, Science, Art and Craft, Music, Physical Education and Sex Education. Although learning is characterized as being largely self-chosen and guided discovery, there is hardly any consideration of the possible integration of subjects. The section entitled 'Flexibility in the Curriculum' discusses project work and centres of interest but there is no attempt to suggest practical principles for integration, except through presenting short case study examples of how children developed a topic or theme. The only general comment is at the end of that section: 'Integration is not only a question of allowing time for interests which do not fit under subject headings; it is as much a matter of seeing the different dimensions of subject work and of using the forms of observation and communication which are the most suitable to a given sequence of learning.' (Para. 542, p. 199). However, in the section 'Use of the Environment' following this, it is suggested that study of the environment is another useful means by which the curriculum can be integrated; again there are a number of suggestions for teachers and some examples of children's work. But nowhere does the report offer a reasoned account of integration. Instead there is a referring back to the 'starting with the child' position, with curriculum content being chosen to resource the kinds of explorations which Eisner termed educational encounters.

This equivocal attitude to curricula is characteristic of child-centred thinking and practice. The Plowden Committee adopted a received view of the primary curriculum by discussing it in terms of subjects it traditionally included without considering the implications of a subjects-based curriculum for the organization of teaching and learning. There is an implicit argument that the subjects are resources for learning to be drawn upon rather than as hard-edged curriculum areas to be presented to children but this is never dealt with systematically and explicitly. The committee is following a well-trodden path in emphasizing the child-centred nature of education, and taking a superficial view of the content of teaching and learning: this tension between learning and curricula is central to child-centredness. Dearden has pointed out that Dottrens, in an international comparative study, identified three hundred and fifty-two subjects being taught in primary schools in various countries, so seeing the curriculum as being made up of separate subjects, whatever these might be, seems to be established primary practice. The notion of subjects being content-pools to be drawn on by teachers in answer to the learning needs of their children is over-simple if it is not clear what a subject is, why these particular subjects have been selected to represent a primary school curriculum, and what teachers would need to know about them if they are to fulfil their teaching functions. So, the committee has not produced anything that can be described as a theory of knowledge or epistemology for the primary curriculum. In not doing so it demonstrates the ambivalence to planning and curriculum development which is inherent in child-centredness. Given this, attempts to change the curriculum are likely to be seen either as irrelevant or encroaching on the teacher's prime responsibility, which is to detect children's educational needs through shaping, directing and resourcing their interests. It is consistent with this line of thinking that projects such as Nuffield Junior Science and Science 5–13 are strong on methods, organization and resourcing but tend to avoid treating science as a discipline, by taking a 'science is all around you' viewpoint.

These late 1960s' concerns are still very much part of the primary education scene even though the 1970s can be seen as more curriculum than child-centred and was a time of intense curriculum development. The DES survey, *Primary Education in England* (1978), raised a number of questions about the curricular needs and deficiencies of teachers which will be discussed later here, but important among them was the lack of 'match' between teachers' curriculum understanding and children's needs and abilities. The curriculum renewal movement in the 1970s gave way in the 1980s to a concern for the need for teachers to be able to demonstrate and prove their professional competence. Since part of this shift in focus arose from events such as the William Tyndale inquiry, which helped to consolidate public doubts about child-centredness in practice, teachers have tended to move away from issues about methods and are becoming more concerned with the content and planning of the primary curriculum at school and classroom levels. Someone returning to a primary school he or she knew in the 1960s or early 70s might well find that in comparison with then there is a greater stress on the need for guidelines in the different subjects and activities of the curriculum for the whole school to use, more attention being paid to children's attainments and the measuring and recording of these, and, in general, a more organized and formal 'feel' about the school. Ironically, the smaller classes brought about by falling rolls which progressive teachers argued as being necessary to the full development of child-centred methods, have enabled teachers in this new climate to be more organized, more efficient, and more formal.

Curriculum and method

It is a further question, of course, as to how far the focus of ideological debate, as distinct from practice in schools, has shifted in the past fifteen years. Alexander (1981), for example, draws attention to 'the continued dominance in primary debate between "child-centred" and "subject-centred" learning.' This is likely to continue in a situation where little has been resolved regarding good practice. It also focusses on an attendant issue, the lack of a distinctive primary school identity, though, as argued, this is perhaps more a characteristic of the junior school. The nursery and infant schools have established identities in terms of a range of practices about which there is no longer any substantive dispute, at least among teachers. Historically, infant schools and departments were outside the Code regulations which allowed a freer development of method and curriculum. The junior departments were subject to a succession of Codes published up to 1937 which in effect spelt out their curricula and developments in methods and organization. There is still in many junior schools an emphasis on basic skills learning, adherence to a mainly subjects-based curriculum and the prevalence of much whole class formal teaching, and possibly a stronger insularity compared with infant schools. Some of this is changing as schools increasingly are reorganized into combined infant and junior schools as a result of falling rolls.

There is also an inevitable tension between respecting children's educational needs higher up in the junior school and preparing them for secondary education. This remains in spite of major curriculum and organizational changes in the lower schools of many large comprehensives, with moves towards integrated studies and team and mixed ability teaching.

If the curricular needs of primary children, apart from the general recognition of the centrality of basic skills, have yet to be settled, then methods have been widely criticized sometimes with little understanding of what they are. The media coverage of the William Tyndale affair revealed a layman's distrust of what were seen as progressive methods, either because they were not understood, or because there was widespread, instinctive belief in the formal and often restricting methods used in primary schooling for previous generations. The Black Paper authors mounted an ideological campaign against progressive methods during the 1970s but there have been more reasoned appraisals such as Dearden's (1967; 1968; 1976) which have important implications for curricular thinking and practice. Dearden is particularly concerned with types of discovery-based learning and the expectations teachers have of these. He distinguishes between three versions or models of discovery: the pre-school model, abstractionism, and problem-solving. The first is very much unstructured exploration with the assumption, Dearden claims, that children will learn important concepts, for instance about mathematics and science, in the process. It is very much the 'science is all around you' approach in which children come to understand key concepts simply by engaging in experiment and play. The teacher's role is to try to plan experience by structuring the environment of the classroom in such a way that discoveries will be made. Dearden's main objection to this is that unless a child has some conception of aspects of mathematics or science he will be unable to recognize mathematical or scientific principles. While this form of exploration is important for children, it is essentially limited in what can be achieved through it, though many teachers, especially in infant classes, make ambitious claims for it.

The abstractionist account is a developed version of the pre-school model. Abstractionist learning dates from John Locke in the seventeenth century, with the contention that the mind was a 'tabula raza' or blank slate, and that knowledge could only come from observation of the physical world through which impressions would be imprinted on the mind. Its discovery learning version is that through exploring the properties of certain structural materials, for example, a child will come to understand – will abstract – principles which his teacher intends him to discover. Dearden's main objection is the logical and practical impossibility, or at least unlikelihood, of this happening.

When a teacher presents a child with some apparatus or materials, such as Cuisenaire rods, Dienes blocks or an assortment of objects on an investigation table, he typically has in mind some one particular conception of what he presents in this way. But then the incredible assumption seems to be made that the teacher's conception of the situation somehow confers a special uniqueness upon it such that the children must also quite inevitably conceive of it in this way too, even though they may not even possess the concepts involved. In some mysterious way, a special potency is thought to inhere in teaching apparatus such that if children play with it or manipulate it, significant experiences must be had, and important concepts must be abstracted. *(Dearden 1967, pp. 145-6)*

This belief seems to derive from two main sources: first, the belief that rather than just tell children something it is more effective to embody that thing in concrete examples of it. But how can a child perceive that thing through experience of a concrete example if he lacks a prior understanding of what would count as an example? Many teachers, for instance, provide their children with number apparatus which embodies number relationships from 1 to 10. If the children do not have some conception of '1 to 10' it is hard to see how they can arrive at that particular set of number relationships. Likewise, teachers often try to teach the general properties of triangles by getting children to make a number of different triangles, cut the corners off, and stick them together on a sheet of paper, so that they produce a straight line which represents 180 degrees. The intention is that children will abstract the general point, that triangles are three-sided figures all of whose angles add up to 180 degrees from the specific and individual triangles they are working with. Some children will make this generalization quickly, others slowly, and others not at all.

The second source, Dearden suggests, derives from research into concept formation and a confusion between what is purposeful inquiry and what is abstracting. This view of discovery learning is held by many teachers and was endorsed by the Plowden Committee. As well as the examples given it is evident in graded reading schemes where a page of text is placed next to a picture, with the apparent assumption that children will be helped to grasp the print by scrutinizing the picture. Dearden's third model, problem solving, does give teachers a number of roles, from instructor to guide to provider of materials:

The teacher does not 'provide experiences' but *guides* experience, by the subtle use of language, towards learning something that is regarded as educationally valuable. *(Dearden 1967, p. 151)*

In summary, Dearden questions the blanket role which various forms of discovery are claimed to have in schools. He concludes that not everything can be left to discovery; there is a place for teachers to tell and instruct and demonstrate if these means are more effective in promoting learning than getting children to discover.

The curriculum planning implications of discovery approaches could work against change taking the form of developed projects and schemes. The role of the teacher is such that child-knowledge is crucial and to be aimed for, and teacher-knowledge in the form of schemes and projects could be seen as impositions on children, constraining their drive to find out through discovery. A naive or extreme interpretation of this approach would be to accept what children have discovered because it is by its very nature superior to what the teacher can contribute from his or her understanding. The act of discovery rather than what is discovered is important because children are trying to find out for themselves in a 'natural' way. In this type of classroom climate there is the danger that false discoveries will be accepted for motivational reasons, since telling a child that he is wrong will dampen his enthusiasm, and for the pedagogical reason that the process is more valuable than the product. Yet a false discovery is a contradiction in terms and ultimately a disservice to children since they have been given to believe that false information is correct.

Another more general influence on the curriculum is inherent in the hierarchical organization of education arising from an ideology of school knowledge which elevates academic and vocational study. In the public's eyes and in many teachers', there is a clear pecking order deriving from the age range of children in different types of schools, and hence their curricular requirements and aims. Thus, infant and nursery schools are the least important and secondary schools the most. Junior schools are all too prominent as being a preparation for the real business of education in secondary schools. It is an approximate gauge, with proximity to adulthood, publicly examined learning and the world of work being the criteria. In this view the secondary curriculum is seen as problematic, with debates over the need for early specialization in subjects clashing with arguments for a better-grounded general education. Lawton (1969; 1973; 1975) has criticized the secondary curriculum for lacking coverage and balance; arguments and proposals for curriculum commonality in secondary education have been developed by him and through the range of DES and HMI policy and discussion papers published since 1977. The subject basis of secondary schooling has been under attack for a number of years with moves towards integration in areas such as the sciences and humanities. Also there is the barely tacit hierarchy of subjects with its distinction between 'pure' subjects with mathematics at the top and 'applied' subjects like home economics at the bottom. Preparation for work and for further study are the main influencing factors in the current debate over what kind of curriculum is desirable for the 14–19 age range; they highlight a deeper issue, whether the secondary school should be more concerned with preparing the young for economic viability through vocational studies or initiating them into the social values and public forms of thought through the traditional subject disciplines.

Until the HMI paper, *A View of the Curriculum*, was published in 1980 little had been said about the primary curriculum in the discussion and policy-making papers published in the aftermath of the Great Debate. The implication was that substantive questions had been settled and that there was an agreed common core made up of basic skills learning in language and mathematics, what might be termed social and moral learning, and a range of acceptable choices so far as other activities were concerned. It is significant that the Inner London Education Authority's document on the curriculum published in 1981, *Curriculum 5–16*, distinguished in its discussion of the primary years between core activities such as language, mathematics, aesthetic development and physical education, which are called 'fundamental elements' and what is called 'the wider curriculum' which is 'a broadly based area of experience and enquiry'. How far this line of thinking is due to the Plowden seamless cloak of knowledge view of the primary curriculum and how far to the traditional preoccupation with teaching methods and classroom organization is hard to say.

Contrasted with this tacit agreement about shape and content is the work of the Schools Council from the late 1960s to the present day, during which time virtually all curriculum activities in the primary curriculum from early childhood education to the junior and middle schools have been rethought through development projects. The impact of these on schools has been patchy, with piecemeal rather than organized change resulting. Project teams established during this period of curriculum renewal were funded typically for three or four years; their membership usually included teachers seconded to the team as field officers. The earlier part of the period was very much the age of the curriculum expert and the idea of school-based curriculum development did not become prominent until the late 1970s when many of the large projects had ceased and further developments were being curtailed by lack of finance. With this development, the notion of the teacher as researcher into his or her own classroom, which Stenhouse has argued for, started to become more of a necessity for curriculum change than an alternative to the large-scale project approach. The concept was at the focal point of the Ford Teaching Project with which Stenhouse was associated, and there has been subsequent interest in action research methodology in classroom-level inquiries carried out by teachers, for instance as documented by Nixon (1981). Research studies such as ORACLE into classroom processes, which is discussed in more detail in the next chapter, is providing valuable material on how teachers perceive their professional responsibilities and roles, but with the full curricular implications yet to be worked out.

Summary

Primary education in Britain has a fairly recent history and its development is partly a reaction against the elementary system and its ethos and partly the result of a reconsideration of the nature of childhood in an educational context. There is a clear direction towards placing the child at the centre of the educational process which can be seen as an ideology in making. Child-centredness is by no means borne out fully in practice though it continues to have a pervasive effect on teachers.

Dewey and Piaget can be seen as the key figures in the development of the basic rationale of child-centredness. Dewey was particularly concerned with pedagogy seen in terms of children's growth, in the context of the society in which they develop. The curriculum planning implications are that a subjects-based curriculum is unsatisfactory because it is alien to the way in which children perceive the world. A fundamental child–curriculum polarity can be established if the curriculum is interpreted in subject terms because there will be no organic connection between it and children's experiences. Piaget's influence comes not from a concern for schooling but through his detailed research into aspects of human development. This had the effect of emphasizing children's individuality and the need for individualized curricula to meet children's needs. Piaget was essentially an epistemologist concerned with the nature of the knowledge children acquire about the world at different stages in their development. Though there are problems in translating his account of knowledge acquisition to educational settings, Piaget has been co-opted in support of a range of views about learning in child-centred situations. These include, for instance, views about learning readiness, in which children's interests have been taken to be more important than data about maturation as evidence of readiness.

The Plowden Report is the most developed public statement on child-centredness with considered views on the nature of learning and its implications for teaching, classroom organization and the curriculum. There are inconsistencies in the reasoning, especially in the committee's treatment of the curriculum: the argument that children's learning does not fit into subject categories does not sit easily with a curricular analysis which is conducted in terms of the separate nature of subjects. Again, this raises fundamental questions which are still being debated about the nature of child-centred compared with subject-centred education. But if there is the impression that the content of the primary curriculum has been settled, there are still questions at different levels of informedness about primary teaching methods. The William Tyndale inquiry demonstrated the public's distrust of what are seen as progressive methods, and the Black Papers mounted an ideological campaign against them throughout the 1970s. Dearden on the other hand offers a more reasoned appraisal through his typology of discovery methods, the pre-school model, abstractionism and problem-solving.

What remains is a basic tension between child-centred methodology and curriculum development, since the latter implies a systematized curriculum which superficially, at least, is at odds with discovery methods. A more general influence derives from the hierarchical organization of education in which primary schools are less valued than secondary schools with consequently less attention being paid to their curricular needs. This is evident in the range of DES and HMI papers published since 1977. In contrast, the Schools Council has mounted curriculum development in virtually every primary curriculum area. What has emerged from this sustained attempt at development is the notion of the teacher as curriculum researcher which is to be seen as a future focal point for curriculum change. While classroom research studies such as ORACLE are producing material on how teachers perceive and exercise their roles, the curricular implications of this material have yet to be worked out.

Further reading

Bruner, J. (1968), *Toward a Theory of Instruction*, New York: Norton
Developmental psychology applied to the planning of children's learning.
Dearden, R. (1976), *Problems in Primary Education*, London: Routledge and Kegan Paul
An analysis of the ideology and practices of child-centredness.
Peters, R. (ed.) (1969), *Perspectives on Plowden*, London: Routledge and Kegan Paul
·A critique of aspects of the report.

3. Classroom processes and curriculum planning

The ORACLE Study

The concept of the teacher as researcher into classrooms is established in the literature though it cannot be claimed yet that a majority of teachers operate with this view in mind. It is linked conceptually to research into classroom processes which seeks to reveal the structural patterns of classrooms and the processes at work within these. Such investigations can have important implications for curriculum development and organization. Research-based teaching implies that curriculum research and development becomes an essential part of a teacher's role in the classroom and possibly the school. This is another view of curriculum development, contrasted with the curriculum developer as curriculum specialist notion embodied in the large-scale projects of the kind launched by the Schools Council in the 1970s. Stenhouse (1975) claims that:

the uniqueness of each classroom setting implies that any proposal – even at school level – needs to be tested and verified and adapted by each teacher in his classroom. The ideal is that the curricular specification should feed a teacher's personal research and development programme through which he is progressively increasing his understanding of his own work and hence bettering his teaching.

To summarise the implications of this position, all well-founded curriculum research and development, whether the work of an individual teacher, of a school, of a group working in a teachers' centre or of a group working within the coordinating framework of a national project, is based on the study of classrooms. It thus rests on the work of teachers.   *(p. 143)*

He discusses this form of teacher-initiated research by considering the Ford Teaching Project in which teachers observed their own classroom performance through a triangulation technique which combined their own observations, the observations of a teacher colleague and the views of pupils.

A wider frame of reference is provided by the ORACLE research project, the acronym meaning Observational Research and Classroom Learning Evaluation, based at the University of Leicester. This was the first large-scale observational study of primary school classrooms to be carried out in Britain. It takes stock of the developments in primary education thought and practice which were influenced by the Plowden Report. The focal point of the study is the patterns of teaching and learning observable in teacher–pupil interaction, how different styles of teaching can be deduced from these, and the linkage between distinctive teaching styles and the differing curricular culture of classrooms. The researchers identified four basic teaching styles, or rather, three distinct styles and a fourth which had several variations. They are as follows:

Style 1   individual monitors
Style 2   class inquirers
Style 3   group instructors
Style 4   style changers

The last of these was divided into three sub-styles: *4a* infrequent changers, *4b* rotating changers, *4c* habitual changers. Since these are the major reference points for the research and relevant here, it will be useful to summarize them:

Individual monitors: This was the largest group, comprising 22.4 per cent of the sample. The main characteristics are a low level of questioning and a high level of non-verbal interaction between teachers and children, mainly consisting of monitoring individual children's work. Learning tasks are individualized through graded worksheets, cards and texts and the teacher's main task is to work with individual children in advising, instructing and eventually marking their work. This is done either by rapidly moving round the class or by sitting at the teacher's desk with queues of children awaiting attention.

Class inquirers   This group comprised 15.5 per cent of the sample. Whole class teaching was the main characteristic with an emphasis on teacher-directed learning and a high level of verbal communication both with the class and individuals with an emphasis on factual information and problem-solving.

Group instructors   These represented 12.1 per cent of the total. Again there is a high degree of teacher-structuring of learning and considerable verbal interchange with a mixture of information-giving and open questions. The researchers suggest that this type comes nearest to the Plowden model of the primary teacher with the strong emphasis placed on group organization.

Style changers   These represent 50 per cent of the sample. Infrequent changers, of which there were 10.3 per cent tended either to group children by friendship or ability but made occasional changes when they perceived the need to change their teaching tactics. Rotating changers of which there were 15.5 per cent organized a form of integrated day in which the groups moved from one activity to another in rotation throughout the day. Time was allotted equally to all curriculum activities and the children moved in groups from one to the next according to the time allowed. Habitual changers, of which there was the high proportion of 24.2 per cent, made frequent changes, which were often unplanned, between group and whole class teaching.

The two main findings of the ORACLE research are that, first, contrary to critics of primary school practice, progressive teaching methods in the Plowden interpretation of these hardly exist, though schools in the past fifteen or twenty years have adopted a considerable range of types of classroom organization. Second, there has been little curriculum change:

in spite of widespread claims in the mass media, by industrialists, and by Black Paper propagandists, the general pattern of the traditional curriculum quite certainly still prevails, and has not changed in any fundamental way, let alone vanished. Such claims appear to have been founded on mythology. It may, perhaps, be argued that the traditional curriculum was in fact largely abandoned in the late 1960s and early 1970s and has now shifted back; but this view cannot be supported by the evidence from research studies. By the 'traditional curriculum' we mean a central focus on skills relating to literacy (language) and numeracy (mathematics). *(Galton, Simon and Croll 1980, p. 155)*

The research team found that in the vast majority of cases there was ordered and purposeful learning which again is contrary to the claims made about the prevalence of chaos and free-for-all: their typical pupil was working effectively for 58 per cent of the time; for a further 12 per cent he was involved in activities such as fetching apparatus or sharpening a pencil, tasks which were necessary to maintaining learning. The typical pupil also spends 4.3 per cent of his time in direct contact with his teacher, asking questions and waiting for his work to be checked, for instance. For 16 per cent of his time the pupil is distracted, that is, not ostensibly working. Active disruption amounted to 0.1 per cent and 'horseplay' to 0.2 per cent. In the approximately 9 per cent remaining of his time, the pupil was partly rather than fully involved in his work. The researchers' analysis of the curriculum bears out their claim that it takes a traditional form, in their terms, in the majority of classrooms, and perhaps is static. The major activities are language and mathematics with a third of the available teaching time being given to each. Mathematics tends to be broken down into number work, practical mathematics and abstract mathematics, while language is composed of reading, writing, oral English and creative writing. The remaining third is devoted to what is termed 'general studies' which includes project and topic work and art and craft. The observations however do not include such out-of-class activities as games, physical education, television lessons and religious education when given in assemblies. So, what the researchers were able to deduce about curriculum coverage conforms fairly closely to the ILEA distinction between the basic and the wider curriculum and also with DES and inspectorate views expressed in such documents as *A View of the Curriculum* (1980).

This seems to bear out what is being argued here, that there is a sense in which the primary curriculum appears to have been settled, in contrast to the secondary curriculum; no substantive questions remain to be asked about it in the eyes of both teachers and the inspectorate.

The research also revealed that the typical pupil spends over 20 per cent of his time on writing of some sort and 14.8 per cent on topic and project work, with science and nature study taking 4.4 per cent. Oral English occupied only 2 per cent of teaching time.

Clearly there is a close relationship between the way a teacher perceives his or her teaching role and how learning is organized in individual classrooms. But while there are striking differences in teaching style and consequently organization for learning, there seems to be general agreement about what constitutes the primary curriculum. The researchers go into considerable detail in identifying and analysing teaching style but the ways in which it influences the range, content and balance of what is taught and learned might have been treated in more depth and detail. Only the basic skills are examined in trying to find out whether particular styles produced better learning. A futher dimension here has to do with the children's temperament and how this affects their learning when they are in contact with a teacher who expresses a particular style. It is arguable that the temperament range in a class is as important, as is demonstrated learning ability among individual children, since the ways in which children are grouped, or group themselves, have a direct effect on the climate of a classroom.

The study identified four pupil types. These are as follows:

Type 1: Attention seekers   These amount to 19.5 per cent of the sample. These children co-operate on classwork for most of the time but are characterized by the way in which they seek contact with the teacher. They are more likely to be observed waiting for the teacher, moving round the class or out of the base areas, than members of other groups.

Type 2: Intermittent workers   These comprise 35.7 per cent of the sample. They have high levels of contact with other children but low level with teachers. Although they work for about two thirds of the available time, they are liable to be involved more than other types in conversations and other distractions and go out of their way to avoid the teacher.

Type 3: Solitary workers   These make up 32.5 per cent of the sample. They do not interact much with other children and have little to do with their teachers. They tend to remain in their places or base areas and to get on with their work, whatever the level of the task set.

Type 4: Quiet collaborators   These comprise 12.3 per cent of the sample. Their chief characteristic is that their main contact with the teacher is as members of a group or of the whole class.

This typology raises interesting questions as to how far different teaching styles might develop or produce particular pupil types, or whether these are so much rooted in individual psychology that different regimes have little impact on them. It is likely though that some types will function better in particular regimes than others, though the researchers are tentative about this:

The relationship suggested in the previous chapter between teaching tactics and pupil behaviour was seen as a two-way interactive process: tactics may influence behaviour and behaviour may affect tactics. The presence of a high or low proportion of any pupil type in a class may be the result of using a particular style of teaching but it is also possible that the teacher adopts the style as a response to certain pupil behaviours. *(Galton et al. 1980, p. 147)*

Teachers as researchers

The material from the ORACLE work probably raises more questions than it answers but what is clear from it is that while primary teachers have a received view of the curriculum, they develop teaching styles which are distinctive to them as individuals. These styles influence the way the curriculum is patterned and presented in classrooms. But this is very much teaching from the educational researchers' perspective. The observational approach used in this kind of study has been criticized for the reductionism which is likely to result, in Stenhouse's words, from trying to make a science from an art. What he argues for is collaboration between teachers and researchers on classroom processes research which will have the intention of improving teachers' performances. Through the experience, teachers would be able to acquire the necessary research skills which would enable them to enquire into aspects of their teaching. Stenhouse is adamant that teachers as a matter of course engage in such research-based teaching since it is the main means by which techniques can be improved. But while the methodological skills of observing and recording can be learned, there is the problem of subjectivity: how far are teachers likely to be able to accept the findings as being conclusive and having implications for their practice? Stenhouse seems to see the subjective element as a strength rather than a weakness:

> Any research into classroom must aim to improve teaching. Thus any research must be applied by teachers, so that the most clinically objective research can only feed into practice through an interested actor in the situation. There is no escaping the fact that it is the teacher's subjective perception which is crucial for practice since he is in a position to control the classroom. *(Stenhouse 1975, p. 157)*

This may be so but the strain of living with the results and the possible damage to self-images is likely to limit the number of teachers who are willing to accept the full professional implications of working in this way. Teachers may well ask what is in it for them, what assurance is there that they will retain control over their own teaching situations since the results of such research could have reverberations beyond their classrooms in the present climate of accountability.

A generally accepted and basic fact about teaching is that teachers are uneasy about being observed, and moving from being observed to participant observation and recording is a big step. There are various ways round this, such as pairs of teacher colleagues collaborating in observation in order to gain mutual support and self-confidence. It means breaking down the traditional isolation of the teacher operating in his or her own classroom which is not to be underestimated as a practical barrier. But it remains a teacher's responsibility in this action-research framework; conventional researchers are likely to be distancing themselves from particular observations in the need to see what is generalizable in their desire to formulate theories of teaching, for instance. There is, as Stenhouse maintains, a need for a general theoretical language, a structure in which to locate such observation, and it is the work of the professional researcher, not the teacher, to focus on this. Through such a framework, a number of case studies might be built up from observational research, as in medicine, and these could be the instruments for investigating the linkage between style, organization and curricula. While the ORACLE team was concerned mainly with teaching styles derivable from observation of processes, Stenhouse believes that the most appropriate and productive area for teacher research is the curriculum. Among projects which have self-monitoring schemes are the Bruner-inspired Man a Course of Study (MaCOS) which includes a classroom observation checklist, and Stenhouse's Humanities Curriculum Project which pioneered this approach in Britain.

The Ford Teaching Project

Reference has already been made to this project which was the first major attempt to develop a research approach to teaching and to explore the possibilities of action research, as well as being concerned with more conventional research tasks. The action research tasks for teachers were:

1   To identify and diagnose in particular situations the problems which arise from attempts to implement inquiry–discovery approaches effectively, and to explore the extent to which problems and diagnostic hypotheses can be generalised.

2   To develop and test practical hypotheses about how the teaching problems identified might be resolved, and to explore the extent to which they could be generally applied.

3   To clarify the aims, values and principles implicit in inquiry–discovery approaches by reflecting about the values implicit in the problems identified. *(Elliott and Adelmann 1976, p. 49)*

The project directors' intention from the beginning was to involve teachers fully in the research and not to draw what they saw as an artificial distinction between teachers and researchers. The project involved forty teachers from twelve primary and secondary schools. In each school, teams of two to four teachers were made up, drawn from different subject areas in the case of secondary teachers. Through these groups, individual support could be generated and in-school team meetings held through which the project would be developed. The schools were then divided into three sub-groups, each consisting of three or four primary and secondary schools in the same area and having access to a local teachers' centre in which there were twice-termly meetings. The intention here was to explore the extent of generality of the approaches being developed and to set up groups which would not be over-dependent on the project team. Three workshops were held for all teachers during the project.

Within this framework a number of procedural principles operated which very much convey the ethos of the project team and the atmosphere of the project. These had to do with the control and conditions under which other teachers would have access to individual teacher's documentation; the degree of control that head-teachers would need to have over the documentation, the principle that all classroom information except pupils' responses should be made accessible to teachers concerned; that teachers would control the project team's access to their classes; and that pupil interview material would be available to others only if pupils themselves released it.

The methodology used for this kind of self-assessment was triangulation. A form of this was developed whereby the observations of teachers in their own classes were monitored by an independent observer and by pupils' observations. Such a plan where pupils have an active role is, of course, potentially threatening to teachers:

The main problem in the monitoring of teacher performance is the threat and anxiety it induces in people who are used to working in isolation, free from the scrutiny of all their pupils. The anxiety is often well founded. External monitors have often made strong evaluations of teachers on the basis of limited understanding of the contexts in which they work and they have tended to use these evaluations in ways which have been harmful rather than constructive for the teacher's professional self-development. *(Elliott 1978, p. 18)*

To reduce the potential threat of triangulation to teachers, it was suggested that a series of stages should precede it, with the teacher early on being helped to collect information about his or her action patterns through keeping a diary or tape recordings, personally analysing the results, and then introducing an observer who with the teacher carries out a second analysis of the data. Finally, triangulation is introduced with the observer interviewing pupils and obtaining their accounts. All three accounts of the period of observation can then be compared and conclusions drawn from them. The project has succeeded in establishing a network of teachers and researchers based at the Cambridge University Institute of Education. This Classroom Action Research Network (CARN) is both developing the original aims and groundwork of the project and providing a forum for teacher and researcher members.

While the classroom observation movement as typified by the Ford Teaching Project has been aimed at teacher development, this sort of investigation also has a potential connection with the accountability movement through its self-assessment nature. Clearly, the distinction between development and assessment is in terms of how the information is used and by whom. Self-evaluation can be translated into self-assessment, an acknowledgement and an extension of professionality but also a stick to beat teachers with. Folk memories of the Elementary Codes are still strong enough for the second interpretation to be feared, especially if local authorities harness self-assessment techniques to a crude performance-objectives view of teacher accountability.

At the same time, the action research approach as an instrument for teacher development is particularly attractive because of its emphasis on finding answers and solutions which can be used, and for this reason a variety of projects of different scales are in operation. The Open University with the Schools Council began *Curriculum in Action* as a continuing education course for teachers, and it takes the teacher as classroom researcher as its basis.

Participant observation is the main method with teachers using a range of techniques to collect and analyse data. The rationale for the course is not elaborated; the emphasis is on inducting teachers quickly into the task of observing systematically the processes of which their teaching is one aspect.

We have adopted the title *Curriculum in Action: an Approach to Evaluation* because you will be asked, throughout the course, to investigate and make decisions about the curriculum as it is experienced in your classroom. Teachers are constantly making on-the-spot decisions about their work and the approach to evaluating the curriculum developed throughout this course should help you to improve your existing classroom skills and to apply them more systematically. As a result, you will be able to obtain and make use of a greater amount of richer information about your work. All subsequent decision making about the curriculum will thus be more firmly based. *(Block 1: An Approach to Evaluation, p. 9)*

As a result of their piloting, the course team arrived at six basic questions needed to provide a structure for teachers' work: what did the pupils actually do; what were they learning; how worthwhile is it; what did I do; what did I learn; what do I intend to do now. The questions are direct and deceptively simple but they imply that teachers will be able to judge and define with insight and subtlety. The act of observation provides material for the investigation of several dimensions of the teachers' work, including the evaluation of their children's learning and their own effectiveness in promoting it, the engagement in epistemological arguments concerning worthwhileness, and the development of reflexivity, that is, the ability to assimilate what they perceive of their own practice and to use this knowledge to refine and improve it.

Nixon (1981) has collected a range of action research studies which are typical of what is being done by teachers. He draws a sharp distinction between this kind of answer-focused work and the traditional notion of research as being carried out at a high academic level by disinterested experts. Since action research is geared to finding solutions to practical problems it has a connection with school-based curriculum development which aims at providing curriculum solutions that apply in specific situations. All but one of Nixon's contributors are teachers, many of whom were involved in the Humanities Curriculum Project on the Ford Teaching Project. This common experience highlights the value of teachers collaborating in work which gives them the skills, confidence and professional attitudes to strike out on their own. The case studies are illustrations of action research being conducted in schools and the ways in which teacher–researchers communicate with each other through networks of various kinds established by the formal framework of a curriculum development project.

Although action research is situation-specific it is likely that similar conclusions will be reached between studies due to the similarities of most teaching situations, especially if these are in the same kinds of schools. Whether findings could be integrated to formulate the theory of teaching which the Ford Teaching Project attempted is a further question since much will be lost in the act of generalizing. There are inherent difficulties in harnessing action research to theory building because the level of generality necessary will not be reached through these means. While the similarities between action research studies can be noted, it is their essential difference which is important. A more practical problem is raised by James and Ebbutt (1981): the need to get the support or at least the approval of colleagues unless one is working entirely in one's own classroom. There is the danger, particularly in this kind of work, of drawing prescriptions for action from inadequate evidence and having to live with the results. Although most of Nixon's contributors had had no research training, they were meticulous in trying to gather information and to relate it to consciously limited questions of practice. A good example of action research is to be found in Brook (1976), where the use of a Wendy House in a reception class in an infant school was studied in order to find out whether the play facilities provided were extending children's play activities. The teacher–researcher circulated a questionnaire to her colleagues to find out what the pattern of usage was in their classes. To gain the children's perceptions she interviewed six children: two who used the house frequently, two occasionally and two hardly at all. They had clear ideas of what for them were the playhouse's possibilities and limitations and she felt able to decide as a result of her research what measures to take in improving the facilities.

There are a number of ways in which researching into the

processes operating in a classroom will involve teachers in curriculum planning. What is clear from the teachers in Nixon's book and the designers of *Curriculum in Action* is that teachers, by changing the conditions of learning in their classrooms, also change the curriculum. The curriculum in a school or a classroom is not something reified or conjured from guidelines or schemes but is the lived experience of both teachers and learners. The curricular implications of 'insider' research are that teachers are directly acting upon those aspects of the curriculum that are both problematic and interesting to them. In researching the interaction patterns they are also exploring the ways in which the hidden curriculum in a classroom interacts with and sustains the actual curriculum. So much of the workings of the hidden curriculum are implicit in teaching and learning that teachers might be unaware of its functioning unless and until they investigate their own and their pupils' perceptions of the classroom climate and how these affect learning and teaching. This kind of understanding is likely to influence the way a teacher organizes the spaces in his or her room, the attention he or she pays to particular groups and individuals and the ways in which aspects of the curriculum are presented to the class as a whole. Engaging in classroom research is a preliminary to engaging in curriculum change at the classroom level, since knowledge of the conditions will frequently point to curricular deficiencies and weaknesses that teachers sense rather than know about. In promoting innovation they are working in their children's best interests and are arguably the only people in a position to bring about curriculum change since they are the only ones in direct contact with 'the situation', in Skilbeck's term. Change might mean modifying what is already there, or bringing in new equipment or materials, or a new view on part of the curriculum. It is a truism that curriculum change does not happen apart from teachers; it is implemented by them and will be on secure foundations if research into what is happening in a classroom leads to clarity about what changes, if any, to make.

Summary

The notion of teacher as researcher, as developed by Stenhouse, is linked to research into classroom processes especially where this has implications for the curriculum. The ORACLE research provides the widest frame of reference here; the focal point for this study is the patterns of teaching and learning which can be observed in a number of classroom processes. Different styles of teaching have been deduced from these and, by implication, the curricular cultures attributable to the different styles. The two main findings are the general lack of curriculum change detectable across the ranges of styles and the presence of a relatively uniform curriculum, and that, contrary to public misgivings, the vast majority of primary classrooms are ordered and purposeful places. The linkage between teaching style and curriculum coverage seems to be similar for all styles, judging by the amount of time children spend on different activities. The research also considers pupil types and what appears to be their different work patterns and relationships with teachers. Although it is tempting to link teacher types to pupil types, the research does not go far into this aspect beyond suggesting that there is a two-way interactive influence.

This kind of work raises a number of issues to do with the possibilities of teachers researching into their own classrooms. Many of these turn on the problematic nature of participant observation, as Stenhouse has suggested. Collaboration with researchers or with other teachers are means by which some of the major problems such as subjectivity and lack of confidence can be overcome. The Ford Teaching Project is the first large-scale attempt to develop a research approach to teaching. It was based on an action research rationale and the roles of teachers and researchers were deliberately blurred. It is a short step from researching into one's own classroom to assessing one's teaching performance; central to achieving this was the triangulation methodology whereby data was obtained from teachers, a non-participant observer and pupils. Three separate contributions to the account of the episode are therefore made. It needs to be noted that such self-assessment can raise folk memories of Payment By Results in the present climate of accountability, but its positive aspect is the way it can extend professionality in the directions which Stenhouse and others have pointed out.

The Ford Teaching Project's work has been complemented by the Schools Council/Open University *Curriculum in Action* course which takes the teacher as researcher as its basis. Both mark the growth of action research as a problem-solving strategy. Nixon has drawn a sharp distinction between this kind of answer-focused research and the traditional notion of research as being esoteric and disinterested. Its curricular implications, for both the actual and the hidden curriculum, are its central concern since all classroom research is a consideration of what is taught and learned; since it is action-orientated it leads to teacher-led change of the kind that Skilbeck has argued for.

Further reading

Boydell, D. (1978), *The Primary Teacher in Action.* London: Open Books
   A guide to recent research on several important aspects of classroom processes.
Galton, M., Simon, B. and Croll, P. (1980), *Inside the Primary Classroom.* London: Routledge and Kegan Paul
Galton, M. and Simon, B. (eds.) (1980), *Progress and Performance in the Primary Classroom.* London: Routledge and Kegan Paul
   Reports on the ORACLE project.
Stenhouse, L. (1975), *An Introduction to Curriculum Research and Development.* London: Heinemann
   Chapters 9–11 develop the teacher as researcher perspective.

4. Primary education and schooling

The social location of primary schools

Much has been said here already about the origins of the primary
school in elementary education and the effects this still has on
teachers' thinking and practice, especially as they perceive children
as pupils, their own roles and how these relate to the primary
curriculum. By implication, this also says much about the social
and educational locations of the primary school. Blyth (1965) considers three traditions in English primary education: the elementary,
the preparatory and the developmental. It is significant that in his
analysis the developmental tradition grew out of the preparatory,
that aspect of schooling which is essentially middle class and fee
paying and therefore of high status and separated from the state-
provided system. It combines with little difficulty both tradition
and innovation; while there is a direct link between preparatory
schools and public schools this does not imply that preparatory
education is confined to the traditional academic curriculum. The
links are more broadly conceived of as being with the fee-paying
sector of secondary education which contains the traditional public
schools along with progressive schools such as St Christophers,
Dartington Hall and Summerhill. The preparatory tradition, too,
contains such figures as Susan Isaacs and Dora Russell as well as
the Froebel-inspired schools for nursery and infant-aged children
which developed in the private sector in the 1880s. It is fairly

recently that progressive views about schooling encapsulating a particular notion of the child as school learner and based on Freudian as well as Piagetian principles found their way into state-provided primary education. This is especially true of junior schools, less so in the case of nursery and infant schools. As Ashton *et al.* (1975) claim:

Until the end of the Second World War, schools catering for the 5–11 age group had a well-established tradition of widely shared practices. Although innovation and change have never been wholly absent from the early years of schooling and many individual schools had a distinctiveness, generally schools tended to be much more alike than is the case now. The purposes of the activities that went on there were readily recognisable, and, probably, generally approved. It was clear that teachers were concerned with competence in a relatively narrow range of skills related to reading, writing and arithmetic, with some formal knowledge of the culture, with proficiency in a few fringe activities in the fields of physical education, art, craft and music, and with the development of particular moral values. The whole of this was conducted within a rather formal framewo·k, reflecting the moral values with which teachers were generally thought to be rightly concerned. *(p. 1)*

In some structural aspects, the scene is not so very different now. The teachers in elementary schools tended to be drawn from the respectable working and lower middle classes; women teachers were required to be spinsters and relinquished their posts if they married; very few teachers were graduates but were trained in colleges which held on to nineteenth-century values and practices concerning the morals of students until relatively recently. The traditions of the pupil-teacher system, a main avenue of upward mobility for bright working-class children from the middle of the nineteenth-century, lingered on well into the twentieth. The social origins of teachers, as Banks (1971) says, is a reflection of the ambiguity of their status. She notes that in a London School of Economics survey of social mobility, elementary teachers were placed alongside news reporters, commercial travellers and jobbing master builders; clearly, below the recognized professions.

Today the status of teachers is still ambiguous and as in the past relates closely to the age range of children they teach and the type of school. Primary teachers are thus seen as being socially and professionally inferior to their secondary school colleagues; factors such as the smaller number of graduates, with the goal of an all-graduate profession still to be achieved, the larger proportion of women in primary schools and the relative lack of promotion prospects compared with secondary teachers combine to depress the status of primary teachers to somewhere not very far away in scale from their predecessors in elementary schools. Such circumstances will have a direct effect on the way primary teachers perceive their roles and the institutions in which they work. Thus it is important to consider in some detail studies of teachers' views about the aims of primary education and how these reflect ideas about children's learning, the composition of the curriculum and the possibilities of curriculum change.

The aims of primary education

Views about aims as discussed here earlier are virtually views about education itself, and, whether or not they are expressed, they underpin an individual teacher's practice, as Boydell (1978) claims:

Each time the teacher responds to that frequent and deceptively simple question: 'What should I do?', she invokes her own philosophy of education with its underlying aims and assumptions. It may have been acquired almost unconsciously during training or worked out with great soul-searching. It may be hazy in parts or even inconsistent. However, it is an integral part of her teaching: what the teacher does is inextricably linked to what she values, to what she regards as good and desirable. *(p. 22)*

The Plowden Report's chapter on the aims of primary education is slightly less than four pages long and is based on open-ended questions put to primary head teachers. The committee however dismissed their replies as being 'little more than benevolent aspiration' since there were many references to the development of individual potential, the need to acquire basic skills and the means to live a full and satisfying life. The committee then turned to professors of educational philosophy and other academics who maintained that there was little value in general statements of aims and that 'a pragmatic approach to the purposes of education was more likely to be fruitful'. What was proposed in the end was a type of checklist which could be used by teachers in their day-to-day work, together with a list of danger signals which would point to bad practice in schools and which would require teachers to ask questions about the value or otherwise of curricular activities. What the committee seems to have tried to do is arrive at a set of objectives rather than aims, but since the nature of an objective was not fully understood by it, the two were confused. What was concluded fell between the two since aims are concerned with values and objectives with practice.

A major study of teachers' views on aims was carried out between 1969 and 1972 based at the University of Birmingham School of Education and funded by the Schools Council (Ashton *et al.*, 1975). The project team worked in co-operation with teacher groups who, through discussion, arrived at a definition and statement of aims. This preliminary work with groups of teachers resulted in a list of seventy-two aims of primary education. It was arrived at with some difficulty. It was found that three stages were needed for teachers to develop aims which were specific enough to apply to primary education and which collectively covered all aspects of primary school activity. The first stage was spontaneously talking about and writing down aims; seventy Midlands primary teachers took part in this through questionnaires following discussion. It was clear from the results that teachers were not used to thinking about aims, and so, to try to refine the statements received, a group discussion approach was used as a follow-up. This focused discussion comprised the second stage. The original seven groups continued and thirty-one more were set up in Devon, Dorset, Northumberland, Durham and North Yorkshire. Through their appointed leaders the groups engaged in focused discussion until they had arrived at a set of aims with which they were satisfied. The meetings were regular and well-attended with all members contributing. Once the first compilations were made, the groups moved to the third stage of structured discussion. The emerging aims seemed to fall into two groups, one to do with aspects of children's intellectual and social development, the other concerning knowledge, skills and qualities. The final seventy-two aims were derived from two thousand aims statements arising from the thirty-eight groups. Selection was made by rejecting unclear and ambiguous statements and those which were duplicated.

These were used as the basis of a questionnaire which was completed by over 1500 teachers in 200 primary schools. While the aims list was not claimed as being definitive, the methods by which it was compiled sought at each stage to respect and follow the lines of thinking being developed in the teacher groups rather than imposing a project group interpretation on discussion. The surveyed teachers were asked to score each aim according to a five-point scale and to indicate any which they felt should not be an aim of primary education. It would have been possible for teachers to score every aim at the highest point. Nearly all agreed that the seventy-two were acceptable for primary education with half being thought to be of utmost or major importance on the scale. Among these thirty-six there were three detectable emphases: one concerned children's personal development which included well-being and cheerfulness, a positive attitude towards school and the development of self-confidence and individuality. The second had to do with social and emotional development, while the third was concerned with the acquisition of basic skills, with reading, oracy and mathematics in that order. Among the other thirty-six aims in the bottom half of the list, in order of importance, were virtually all curriculum activities other than basic skills – expressive arts including music, physical education, religious education, sex education, science and knowledge of a second language. Also in the bottom half were higher-order skills such as being critical and discriminating, being able to form a considered opinion, understanding one's emotions, and playing a part in one's own development, though all of these were considered to be valid aims of primary education.

What is interesting here are the characteristics of teachers contributing to this ordering. There were very few differences between men and women teachers; married teachers tended to place more value on basic skills-learning than unmarried. Personal levels of education played a part in how importantly the basics were regarded, with graduate teachers ranking them lower than certificated teachers. Additionally, graduates were more sympathetic to informal teaching methods than were certificated teachers. The sample

Curricular aims related to	Personal aims	Social/moral aims
Reading	**Utmost importance** Happiness Individuality Positive attitudes to school	Good behaviour
Oracy Mathematics	**Very important** Outgoingness Confidence Control Purposefulness	Positive attitudes to others Conformity Good work attitudes
Literacy (except reading) General knowledge Religious knowledge	**Less important** Self-knowledge Independence of mind Decision-making	Religion-based behaviour Social effectiveness
Physical education Science and technology Sex education Music Second language	**Not very important**	

(Ashton, Kneen, Davies and Holley, 1975)

Figure 5   *Relative importance of different aims*

tended to fall into two groups according to how the purposes of education were thought to be orientated, with the older, more experienced teachers taking a socially orientated view of education, concerned with integrating children into society through the inculcation of social and personal skills. The younger, less experienced teachers tended to focus on progressive methods and the need to promote personal, social and intellectual individuality. These two groupings have considerable implications for the primary curriculum since they indicate the directions which change might take:

There is a strong 'three Rs' flavour to the aspirations of the societal teachers. They most want children to read fluently, accurately and with understanding. They want them to write clear and meaningful, grammatical, correctly spelt English in legible handwriting. They want children to be able to do arithmetical computations and to cope with the mathematics of everyday situations . . . . Within this same group of aims comes the desire for children to be obedient, industrious, persistent and conscientious . . . .

In sharp contrast are the major aims of the individualistic teachers. Revealingly, the highest loadings within their chosen intellectual group of aims were upon the children making reasoned judgements and choices and forming a considered opinion. Here immediately is the notion of children using their minds in their own way, completely in line with these teachers' basic purpose of enabling children to develop their own attitudes towards society and their own chosen way of life . . . . Related to this area but on a wider scale, these teachers want children to be able to plan independent work, organise their own time, to play a part in their own development by recognising their own strengths and limitations and setting their own goals and, of course to be individuals, developing in their own way. *(Ashton,* et al., *1975, p. 89)*

The latter group was also strongly in favour of expressive and creative activities. Clearly the two groups see primary education in markedly different ways and this also applies to teaching methods with the 'individualistic' teachers favouring progressive, discovery-based approaches and the 'societal' teachers believing that learning should be more formal and teacher-directed. Other research into teachers' views about aims are in general agreement with these results, notably Bennett (1976) in which teachers who were formal in style were close to the 'societal' group and the informal teachers were aligned with the 'individualistic' teachers in the Schools Council study. In general terms, too, the ORACLE work is in accord with these findings.

Models of professionality

The research has a number of implications, particularly for curriculum change. As discussed earlier, the work underlines the emphasis placed on basic skills-learning by a great many teachers. At the same time, there appears to be another large group who hold a more enlightened view of the curriculum and of children as learners. Hoyle (1975) has referred to teachers as being restricted or extended professionals according to their perceptions of role and this is likely to have a bearing on how far a teacher is receptive to the possibilities of curriculum change as a result of reviewing his or her own practice. Restricted professionals are characterized by a high level of classroom competence, being child-centred, having a high degree of skill in understanding and managing children, and deriving personal and professional satisfaction from their relationships with children. They attend practical in-service courses and assess their teaching ability through what is observable in children's learning. Extended professionals take a broader view of their roles in considering them in the contexts of school, community and society. They participate in a wide range of professional activities such as teachers' centres, subject associations and conferences and are concerned with the possibilities of linking theory with practice, as well as having an articulated notion of curriculum planning and evaluation. Stenhouse would like Hoyle's description of extended professionality to include the commitment to question one's own practice systematically, to study one's teaching and to test theory against practice. Not surprisingly he sees the extended professional in terms of his own view of the teacher as curriculum researcher.

It would be naive to equate Hoyle's and Stenhouse's characterizations precisely to the 'societal' and the 'individualistic' teachers of the Schools Council study. Perhaps there is the exception of teachers with higher qualifications who were in a small minority in the survey, and who were significantly in favour of 'progressive' and 'most progressive' teacher roles, in the researchers' terminology. It might be expected that the concept of extended professionality would be applied to such teachers because of their views about the nature of primary education and teachers' roles. In a further exploration of role, the Schools Council study asked teachers not to indicate their agreement or disagreement with statements about different approaches to teaching, but to state their own positions. Here, too, the teachers with higher qualifications were more child-centred and progressive than the others. The researchers raise the question as to whether the pursuit of higher qualifications leads to the adoption of more progressive methods, or whether a belief in these leads to the pursuit of a higher qualification. Whichever, there is an apparent link which further indicates something like extended professionality. The researchers in discussing teachers' roles and how these seem to relate to expressed aims concluded that their findings suggested that there was such a difference of opinion between teachers that this might represent a fundamental cleavage.

Climates for curriculum change

Whether or not proposals for change in a school are accepted depend in the end on whether or not the teachers want them. Though there are various theories about the phenomenon of change, little seems to be known about the change process itself except that it is clear that teachers can hinder or facilitate it since it is they who carry it out in their own classrooms. Extended professionals are likely to have positive critical attitudes towards it while restricted professionals, more mindful of their classroom autonomy, are likely to be more cautious in accepting proposed innovations unless they fulfil recognized and pressing needs in their classrooms. But there is a general problem affecting teachers, which Stenhouse argues is directly related to the problem of classroom control:

Schools are – with the possible exception of the armed forces in war-time – the only institutions taking in a conscript population covering the whole of society. It follows that the school has a considerable problem of morale and control. In an earlier chapter I reviewed work which suggested that the knowledge taught by the school is distorted by control problems. If this is so, curricular changes, in so far as they imply changes in the nature of educational knowledge, threaten the teacher's control habits and thus threaten control. *(Stenhouse 1975, p. 167)*

He argues that order in school is achieved by a delicate balance being effected between those institutional arrangements, and norms for conduct which are termed the 'hidden curriculum': any proposed change which threatens to upset that balance will be resisted on those grounds alone by the majority of teachers, irrespective of how potentially beneficial in fulfilling learning needs that innovation might be. Change is associated with conflict and dissent among colleagues. Stenhouse has secondary schools in minds and probably his own Humanities Curriculum Project, but these circumstances are similar for all types of school. He also suggests that the problem of justifying change to outsiders such as parents can be as strong an influence against change as that of individual teachers trying to adjust to the shift in balance in which some colleagues in a school become more prominent than others. It is this realignment of the scheme of things which particularly affects the maintaining of order. Schools and teachers are apt to take up a certain moral stance towards pupils and parents in which the potential benefits of change for pupils will be balanced against the temporary disruption it causes, with consequences for career, self-images and discipline. Such moral authority can be weakened if there appears to be internal doubts about the reconciliation of innovation and stability.

So far as individual teachers are concerned, Stenhouse claims that innovation brings the threat of temporary incompetence until it has become part of the routine. This strikes at the roots of teachers' instructional roles in that it exposes individual teachers; their collective responsibility for maintaining order and moral authority is threatened by incipient change. The fear of incompetence, real or imagined, is the main cause of the failure of much curriculum development. The idea of curriculum negotiation which MacDonald and Walker (1976) have formulated is an attempt to come to terms with this structural incompetence brought about by change. It also recognizes the ambivalent attitudes which many teachers have about innovation. It is as if the very newness of an innovation should bring with it the assurance of success when it is implemented. Also there is both the sense of competence being recognized when teachers are asked to pilot new curricula, and the sense that if developers expect teachers to expose their authority as teachers to possible challenge, from other teachers and from children, the least that developers should do is produce materials to the point of over-resourcing, to ensure that such risk taking is limited, or worthwhile. There is, of course, the ordinary fear of the unknown about which teachers will feel less insecure if curriculum packages are offered. On the other hand, there is teachers' professional identity to contend with. If they have had little or no say in the design and implementation of the innovation, they are likely to feel that their stake in it is likewise limited. Accordingly, the extent of its success might be limited, or it will fail to take. Teachers' classroom autonomy entails that they will judge what is appropriate for their children, and anything which looks like prejudgement by outside experts will be resented. Perhaps it all comes down to teachers and experts – each role has its legitimate sphere of activity from which it derives its authority and when changes are being implemented it is in the nature of such roles that they intersect and clash.

The ways schools are organized presents further barriers to change. This has been investigated as a supplementary project to the Schools Council's Aims of Primary Education Project recently discussed. The study involved twelve urban primary schools in one local authority and one hundred and twenty teachers. Personal background information about them was obtained; they were then asked to name persons and organizations according to the influence they thought these exerted on what was taught in their schools. The respondents were also asked to rate a number of aims of primary education, some apparent constraints on the achievement of these, and to respond to a range of statements concerned with attitudes to stated aims, curriculum innovation and teaching methods. The researchers' concern was for the de facto or operational curriculum actually taught in the schools, and the study investigated to what extent the teachers' declared aims as general statements of intent were transmitted through the curriculum:

Between intention and action and transaction, there exists a large area of decision and choice, and it is within this area that influences and constraints may be assumed to operate. The aims which count in the education of each and every child are those which effectively shape the *operational curriculum*, and it is on understanding how 'stated' aims are translated into 'operational' aims that this study focuses. *(Taylor, Reid, Holley and Exon 1974, p. 1)*

The teachers distinguished sharply between their schools and their classrooms in terms of what most influenced them, with pupils, parents' needs, and expectations playing a major part in school influences, and the teachers themselves being the most influential factors in their own classrooms. What this indicates is a high degree of expressed autonomy in classrooms but little influence over school decision-making. Professional freedom, then, tends to be exerted in the classroom but not the school. Virtually all the named influences were close to or in the school, with head teachers being influential figures in both school and classroom. Public and general opinion exercise a fairly strong but pervasive influence which is consistent with the moral authority which schools traditionally exert in a community. Teachers do not feel especially constrained, judging from the research; the most common constraints named were size of class, size and design of classrooms, available storage space, provision of materials and ancillary help, and liaison between schools and children's homes. While none of these seriously infringed teachers' autonomy, they conspired to prevent them from achieving their declared aims.

The evidence also suggests that teachers see little value in stating aims. As in the larger research project there is divergence with one group favouring child-centred, experiential approaches which are intuitive rather than overtly planned, and the other group being in support of formal, explicitly planned approaches. The groups are about equal in size. Again, as a single teacher group, they appear to be in favour of stating aims where the whole school is involved but not where their own classes are the focal point. Attitudes towards change are difficult to gauge. There is a belief that what is best in primary education should be retained but that traditional excellence is not sufficient grounds for retaining past practices. The teachers feel that the ways in which change is brought about is more important than whether or not there should be change: procedures are seen to be more important than the decisions which bring them into play. They are divided on whether or not there should be a major curriculum rethink; there is the impression that:

The teacher secures his reward out of what takes place in the classroom and is not greatly concerned with how the school's curriculum is ordered, what its purpose is in detail or whether change in it should take place, so long as he secures to himself a personally manageable and satisfying set of transactions with his pupils. *(Taylor* et al *1974, p. 62)*

The implications of this are that there are unlikely to be wholesale curriculum changes in the form of major reappraisals but that limited, piecemeal innovation is possible and likely. Yet there has been a considerable amount of attempted development over the past fifteen years across the whole curriculum and covering the whole primary age range. Development does not, of course, necessarily result in change. But how much of this has been successful? What counts as success? Hoyle (1975) claims that schools in this country are effective in introducing innovations but bad in maintaining them. 'Creativity', which, in his terms, is the ability to sustain innovation, is related to the school's organization: if the organizational climate is such that possible innovations are considered positively as solutions to problems rather than being threatening to staff, 'tissue rejection' will not take place.

But little is known about the ways in which particular structures produce certain types of climate which favour curricular and organizational change. Perhaps less is known about how climates themselves may by changed. These problems, along with the notion of systematic change and the theory systems it has generated, are worth considering here. Hoyle poses the question: how does the curriculum change? His question concerns systematic planning and what he terms 'drift' which is unplanned. Both he and Miles (1965), who developed the concept of 'organizational health' which can be applied to a school to determine whether or not its climate is conducive to change, perceive curriculum change as being a form of social change. Stenhouse in rejecting this approach prefers to focus on the school personnel; he suggests that 'consult' type decisions made by head teachers are probably the emerging style for whole-school innovation in this country.

But this claim only underlines the importance of trying to identify what it is in one school which predisposes it towards innovation, and what it is in another where innovation is rejected. Hoyle's conclusions are fairly guarded:

This does not assume that innovative schools will indiscriminately adopt anything which is new but that they will adopt some innovations and reject others dependent upon their relevance to the particular needs of the school at a given time. It does assume, however, that some schools are more open to new ideas than others. It also assumes that schools have a collective quality of innovativeness. Ultimately the individual teacher is the 'adopting unit' who will determine the effectiveness of an innovation, and some teachers will have more 'open' minds than others as a function of their cognitive, perceptual and creative skills. *(Hoyle 1969, pp. 385-6)*

He broadly accepts Miles' concept of organizational health as 'a school system's ability not only to function effectively, but to develop and grow into a more fully-functioning system'. He extends Miles' medical metaphor by suggesting that the main problem facing curriculum developers is 'tissue rejection', where an innovation does not 'take' in a school because its social system excludes the possibility of it becoming part of the school's curriculum. What seems to be reasonably well established is that the most significant figure, apart from the class teacher, in determining whether or not innovation will succeed is the head teacher. Halpin's research into school climates has produced a typology of head teachers on a continuum from 'open' to 'closed':

Open: The head is a leader; works hard and thus sets an example; establishes rules and procedures; is prepared to be critical; is flexible in meeting staff needs; morale is high in the school because of a feeling of accomplishment by the staff.
Autonomous: The head gives greater autonomy to staff than an open head; less positive leadership; does not meet social needs as effectively; staff have a sense of task success.
Controlled: Authoritarian head who controls staff closely; works them hard; staff nevertheless respond and gain satisfaction from task success.
Familiar: The head is mainly concerned with establishing a friendly happy atmosphere; little leadership or control exerted; staff morale is diminished through having little sense of task achievement.
Paternal: The head tries to exert control with little effect; busy in the school and this is regarded by staff as interference; the climate is distrusted by the staff who have little sense of task success.

Closed: The head is aloof, impersonal, controlling; no leadership; staff gain little satisfaction either from social relationships or achievements.

Although, on this evidence, the open head is likely to generate a climate most conducive to change, Halpin asserts that little is known about how climates can be changed. Hoyle suggests that if teachers had a greater share in decision-making, schools would be more innovative, but this seems to be contrary to some of the findings resulting from research into teachers' views on aims, as discussed. The reality is that teachers have such considerable classroom autonomy that it would be difficult for all but the most authoritarian head to make teachers accept an innovation against their better judgement or prejudices. Miles, working from American experience, acknowledges the power of teachers over change and suggests a number of strategies for implementing change which stress group rather than individual effort and commitment. They assume that the group is the unit of change, which might be the case in education systems where teachers have less freedom than in Britain. The dilemma in Britain is that unco-ordinated, piecemeal change is possible where individual autonomy is respected, but that school-focused change requires the staff to function as a group: this entails weaker autonomy but stronger professionality.

Models of curriculum change

There is a considerable, if inconclusive, literature on the links between organizational climates and change; likewise, there are several theories which seek to explain the nature of systematized change. Havelock (1971) has developed three models based on American experience which are in general terms translatable to other education systems. They have become the bedrock models of curriculum diffusion along with Schon's three models of curriculum dissemination which complement them. They are derived from research into several hundreds of studies of change in the fields of education, medicine, agriculture and industrial technology. Havelock terms them the *RD and D* model (research, development and

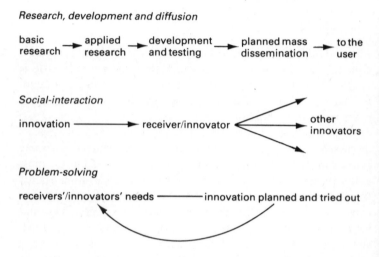

Figure 6   *Havelock: models of planned change (a simplified diagram)*

diffusion), the *social-interaction* model and the *problem-solving* model.

Skilbeck has raised the general question as to whether models of change fit the practical realities; these in their various ways have been influential in reflecting processes of change.

The *RD and D* model makes the assumption that there will be a rational sequence in the design, development and dissemination of an innovation. It follows that the project materials are researched and packaged before the project is disseminated to what are seen as passive and approving consumers. It has been described as the 'agricultural' model since it is like research and development on agricultural testing stations engaged in producing better plants with higher yields for farmers. The rational sequence accords with a behavioural objectives approach towards curriculum planning and was used in the first wave of American curriculum development after Sputnik 1 in 1957. It aims to produce packaged solutions to curriculum problems which are first identified by curriculum experts. The teacher is therefore the passive accepter of teacher-proof curriculum packages; at the core of this model is the notion of the teacher as a technician. Programmed materials which are claimed to be complete in themselves, such as the SRA Reading Laboratory, are the nearest primary curriculum product used widely in Britain to correspond with this view. The teacher launches children on a series of preplanned stages and monitors their attainment at each stage. The package also includes self-assessment procedures which potentially reduce the teacher's instructional role even further.

The *social-interaction* model makes several assumptions, the chief one being that the potential user of an innovation belongs to a network of fellow professionals who will strongly influence his disposition to adopt or reject what is being offered. Informal personal contact is crucial to dissemination with the marketing of products giving way to the conducting of messages in a network. But there is still a donor and recipient view of dissemination in that the teachers receive the flow of ideas from the curriculum experts. The kind of in-service training course that is required before a teacher can use the Man a Course of Study (MaCOS) materials is close to this view, likewise the preparation needed for teachers to act as neutral chairmen in the Humanities Curriculum Project.

The *problem-solving* model retains the donor and recipient relationship, but it does actually start from problems identified by teachers – there is more of the rhetoric of collaboration and sometimes the reality. The main assumption is that innovation is part of a problem-solving process where a particular need is identified by teachers, and curriculum experts devise the solution which teachers put to use.

Schon (1971) proposes three models of the dissemination of innovation. Again, his work does not stem exclusively from education but is based on the study of social systems undergoing change. The *centre periphery* model assumes that the innovation has been designed and is ready to be diffused; the process of diffusion is centrally managed by the inventors of the innovation. Agriculture, medicine and industry provide the basis for this model, and, as with the RD and D model, it suggests curriculum experts designing and marketing packaged solutions for passive teachers. His second model, the *proliferation of centres*, is more characteristic of

large-scale curriculum development. It is based on a trainer of
trainers viewpoint where curriculum experts initiate others into the
use of the innovation, who then set up secondary centres supported
by the central, primary centre. This model most closely resembles
the Schools Council's work when it was funding major national
projects which led to the establishment of local centres for their
diffusion. A problem with this model in practice is that the primary
centre's messages might be misunderstood or repudiated by the
secondary centres, leading to a distortion or debasement of the
original conception of the project. A typical late-twentieth-century
model is Schon's third, the *shifting centres* model, where broad
unsystematized movements take the place of centres. Civil rights,
nuclear disarmament and Black Power have been characteristic
political and social movements. In education, the Educational
Priority Area action research projects resulting from the Plowden
recommendations on educational priority areas in the inner city are
representative, when the brief for a project team was to define the
needs of an inner city area and develop a programme to satisfy these.

MacDonald and Walker's concept of curriculum negotiation is
drawn entirely from project developments in schools. They suggest
five propositions which apply to all projects when they are in the
process of passing from the developers' hands into the teachers'.
These are that all projects are subordinate to schools and will be
adopted or rejected according to how well they fit the school
situation; projects present different images of themselves to different
audiences; because of this there are usually two views as to what the
project 'is', one held by teachers, the other by the project's critics;
there is normally a gap between intent and practice because of this;
curriculum dissemination occurs through a process of negotiation
between the project's sponsors and teachers. They say this about
negotiation:

The thesis can be simply stated as follows: the gap between project intent
and classroom practice is not primarily a matter of miscommunication by
the project or misuse by the teachers. Rather it is a consequence of a series
of 'trade-offs' that are negotiated at each successive point of sale. 'What is
implemented' is much closer to 'what is sold' than is commonly realised.
That this truth is not widely understood is due to an idealised image of the

new curriculum perpetuated by the self-appointed monitors of curriculum innovation. *(MacDonald and Walker 1976, p. 47)*

They further suggest that projects, if they are to 'pass the test', that is, be accepted by the majority of teachers, must have the following characteristics:

1   a 'non-divisive' view of the curriculum needs of the pupils;
2   a high estimate of the achievement of the low-achieving pupil;
3   a fully articulated theory of pedagogy in its content area;
4   a new curriculum that embodies the 'latest' conception of the subject held by university scholars. *(MacDonald and Walker 1976, p. 49)*

Although they use the secondary project 'Geography for the Young School Leaver' as their main case study, these criteria could readily be put against a large-scale primary project such as science 5–13 with only 4 above not fitting well. However, a restatement of what science is for the primary school child was argued forcefully by the project team. There is a down-to-earth flavour about MacDonald and Walker's proposals which make them sound convincing and readily applicable compared with the highly generalized accounts of Havelock and Schon which sound somewhat arid and divorced from classroom realities.

There is also an anti-models argument put forward by Skilbeck (1971) in which he claims that the human activities involved in curriculum innovation are so complex that no one model can contain them even in general terms:

From a review of literature and research I have reached the conclusion that several thousand years of practice, a rather lesser period of theory and a half century of research have not yet yielded a single over-arching strategy for curriculum innovation which rises much above the level of platitude and commonsense. *(p. 29)*

As there are no single solutions, he suggests that we should try to find out how people actually bring about curriculum change so that from this empirical and practical inquiry, some ideas might lead us to general principles. He is concerned with school-based curriculum development because only teachers, in the end, can be responsible for curriculum change. Heads have an interest in it from the point of view of developing whole-school policies, but class teachers have a direct, practitioners' interest in change. Skilbeck also claims that pupils, legitimately, have a view of the curriculum which should be taken account of by teachers. It is notable that he is the only theorist who mentions children, as if the system builders can only conceptualize their schemes at the level of teacher and curriculum developer. There are three reasons, he argues, why teachers are the only legitimate agents of change:

First, of the concept of education itself, as we understand it, of the tradition of values and experience evolved through thought, inquiry and experience. Second, of society, especially of those identifiable forces to which the school owes allegiance: parents, the educational administrative framework, the polity, the economy and so forth.... Third, the teacher is an agent of his own pupils, of their 'best interest' to learn and grow through education. *(Skilbeck 1971, p. 33)*

Teachers are the only ones able to analyse 'the situation' since they are directly responsible for it. He concludes that there are a number of factors which directly affect curriculum change as he understands it, but which do not comprise a system. They are all focused on the analysis of this situation which the teacher alone is in a position to carry out. Strategies will be different for different situations; by nature they are not generalizable.

All this works against Miles's claim that the group and not the individual is the main agent of change. Groups give the sort of mutual support to individuals that they are likely to need when faced with the uncertainties of change. In a school, all, or a significant majority, of the staff need to be supportive of an innovation if it is to take root. Of course the commitment to a systematic approach to change suggests the orderly management of a group rather than the degrees of uncertainty that working with individuals is likely to bring. According to Hoyle (1975), curriculum innovation in primary schools has been unsystematic compared with that in secondary schools:

In spite of the existence of national curriculum projects for primary schools, the transformation has been an informal, relatively unplanned and more or less spontaneous movement. *(p. 342)*

He suggests four reasons. The class–teacher basis and the generalist nature of primary teaching, works against the implementation of planned change. The power of primary heads is amplified because of the greater face-to-face contact they have with their staffs compared with secondary heads. The task of keeping order is claimed to be easier for teachers in primary schools, which on the face of it should ease change. The fact that primary schools are no longer the direct agents for selection for secondary schooling in most local authorities removes an earlier constraint.

Summary

The social and educational location of primary schools in Britain has been influenced by three traditions. The development of primary education has partly been due to a reaction against the elementary ethos. The developmental and preparatory traditions have strong historical ties; together, they began to transform teaching in nursery and infant schools and departments towards the end of the nineteenth century, though junior education has lagged behind. Inevitably, the social location of schools is reflected in the status of teachers. Elementary teachers tended to be drawn from the respectable working and lower middle classes; similar origins and status are to be found among teachers in state-provided schools, and especially primary schools today.

Teachers' status colours teachers' professional self-images and how these are expressed both in practice in classrooms and in their views about the nature and aims of education. It is clear that expressed aims and practice are interdependent. A major study of aims was carried out by the Schools Council. In the early stages, the emerging aims seem to fall into two groups: one to do with aspects of children's intellectual and social development, the other concerning knowledge and skills. The characteristics of teachers in each group formed distinct patterns; the 'individualistic' teachers, who tended to be the youngest and best educated, were in favour of the development of progressive teaching methods and the need to extend personal, social, intellectual and expressive individuality. The 'societal' teachers, who tended to be older and less well educated, valued aims which stressed integrating the young into society and promoting social skills.

The study has implications for models of professionality and especially, in Hoyle's terms, for restricted and extended professionals. The second are likely to be more positive towards curricular and organizational change than the first and to have educational views which extend to values beyond the classroom.

This type of formulation is important for understanding how propitious climates for change arise out of certain conditions obtaining in a school. Stenhouse has commented on the delicate equilibrium which schools need to achieve from a combination of institutional arrangements and aspects of the hidden curriculum. Teachers in the end are the implementers of change; they have to weigh the possible long-term benefits against the temporary disorder and incompetence which threaten while they acquire the skills needed to operate with the innovation. Curriculum negotiation accepts the nature of this weighing-up; teachers will accept innovation if it both promises to solve curricular problems and respects their professional freedom to choose.

But there are numerous internal and external influences on schools which teachers are well aware of and which effectively limit their autonomy to their own classrooms. Head teachers are the crucial figures inside schools and the school's climate will largely depend on the style of leadership exerted by them. In the light of the internal influences especially, the models of planned change advanced by Havelock seem implausible particularly in decentralized education systems. Schon's models of diffusion have an application to large-scale curriculum development, but lack the fine-tuning which might enable them to account for changes in classrooms. Curriculum negotiation, by placing teachers as equal partners alongside curriculum developers, goes some way towards accounting for the phenomenon of change which happens as a result of trade-offs between teachers and developers so that the innovation finally accepted is in a form which is acceptable to both parties. Skilbeck asserts the futility of theorizing; teachers are the sole legitimate agents of change because only they are in a position to assess 'the situation' – their own classrooms.

Further reading

Ashton, P., Kneen, P., Davies, F. and Holley, B. (1975), *The Aims of Primary Education: A Study of Teachers' Opinions*, London: Macmillan Educational.

Taylor, P., Reid, W., Holley, B. and Exon, G. (1974), *Purpose, Power and Constraint in the Primary School Curriculum*, London: Macmillan Educational
Reports of the Schools Council's research into primary teachers' views of the aims of education.

MacDonald, B., and Walker, R. (1976), *Changing the Curriculum*, London: Open Books
Survey of strategies for change including curriculum negotiation.

5. Curriculum development in primary education

The conditions of development

It has been suggested that questions about the content of the primary curriculum have largely been settled and that curriculum development needs to aim at improving the status quo rather than attempt radical innovation. Such documents as the DES survey of primary education, the policy making and discussion documents by the DES and HMI from 1977 have in effect defined content. The position is in contrast to the secondary curriculum where there have been major upheavals caused by the raising of the school leaving age to 16 in 1973, the recent and current debate over curricular relevance for 14- to 19-year-olds, and the long-term and unreconciled academic versus vocational curriculum argument. These have been accompanied by major changes in the structure of secondary education since the publication of the Crosland circular in 1965, requiring all local education authorities to submit their plans for comprehensive reorganization to the DES. Since then comprehensive schools of several different kinds have evolved and are being developed, the debate over tertiary colleges has not been settled and the whole notion of making the curriculum more relevant to adulthood is still being pursued.

In primary schools, the main change is that their selective function began to diminish as comprehensive reorganization grew, and with this there was a general move to unstream in junior schools from the late 1960s. Other changes have been structural on a smaller scale, such as the development of vertical or family grouping, especially in infant schools, and team and co-operative teaching to operate in the combinations of large and small spaces provided in modern open-plan buildings. All of these have had an effect on teaching methods and organization but hardly at all on the curriculum, in spite of the fact that the decade between the mid 1960s and mid 1970s was a concerted period of curriculum development. The ORACLE research revealed a stable and largely static curriculum, likewise the earlier Lancaster study of teaching styles. What then has been the fate of the primary curriculum development work begun by the Nuffield Foundation and carried on by the Schools Council?

The Schools Council for Curriculum and Examinations was established in 1964. Its terms of reference were 'to undertake research and development work on the curriculum, and to advise the Secretary of State on matters of examination policy'. (Lawton, 1980, p. 68) It was funded jointly by the DES and the local authorities and its constitution admitted a majority of teachers on its policy-making sub-committees. It began by identifying six main areas of activity which included the primary school curriculum, the curriculum for the early leaver, the sixth form curriculum, 16+ examinations and the particular requirements of schools in Wales. So far as the secondary curriculum is concerned, the tension between the development of subjects and satisfying examination requirements was largely solved through Mode 3 CSE examinations, with teams for major projects recognizing the need to meet schools' examination needs if their projects were to be acceptable. This in itself has probably reinforced the separate subject nature of the secondary curriculum and its development. Early critics of the Schools Council such as Young (1971) argued that low-status pupils such as early leavers and those in primary schools were being concentrated on at the expense of focusing on the mainstream academic curriculum because political rhetoric demanded attention for these, with the mainstream by implication being left alone. But nearly two hundred projects had been mounted by the Council by the end of the 1970s, covering virtually the whole of the school curriculum. So far as primary education is concerned, it is difficult to judge how effective such development has been in influencing change. The fact that much of it was as subjects-based as the developments in the secondary curriculum reveals the consensus view on content which was adopted. Only one project, the University of Lancaster-based Middle Years of Schooling Project, considered the whole curriculum range for an age group. It stemmed from the Plowden Committee's achievement in concentrating educational thinking about practice and its justification, and a number of subsidiary subject projects were generated from the ground-plan it laid down.

The Schools Council research study, *Pattern and Variation in Curriculum Development Projects* (1973), suggests five broad reasons for the establishment of projects:

response to scientific and technological advance;
response to social changes outside the education system;
meeting special needs not previously catered for by schools;
taking advantage of recent advances in educational or other research;
responses to changes in the education system itself. *(p. 15)*

The primary projects seem to derive mainly from the fourth reason; they did not seek to bring about major changes but to improve on what was already there, but there was still the question of take-up.

The increasing pace of advances in knowledge and social change demands an increasing rate of change in the educational system. Curriculum development projects are a response to this need in a situation where it appears that organized innovation is required to overcome the inertia of the existing system. This inertia is largely a property of teaching materials, teachers' education and experience, and, in some curriculum areas, external examinations. *(Schools Council 1973, p. 16)*

The researchers note that all the primary projects up to date have stressed methods rather than content with the advancement of teachers' professional development in mind. The presentation of projects to teachers has therefore taken the form of emphasizing teaching approaches, such as the case-study examples of good practice in the Science 5–13 teachers' guide, and the emphasis on the development of multimedia materials and apparatus in the Programme on Linguistics and Teaching. The Environmental Studies Project team focused on the use of the school environment as the prime teaching resource for a multidisciplinary area of study comprising geography, history and science. The History, Geography and Social Studies Project was concerned with the development of certain key concepts which teachers would resource according to their local needs and situations. The Art and Craft Education 8–13 Project aimed at improving teachers' practice by making them more knowledgeable and aware of children's creative processes which could be developed and realized through art and craft activities. In taking this general line, the project teams were clearly aware of the Plowden-inspired concern for teaching approaches which respected the child and required the teacher to resource learning by establishing effective learning environments. So the emphasis is not on transmitting a body of knowledge but on inducting teachers into new ways of perceiving an established subject or activity and on helping them to become better resourcers of learning. For example, the Science 5–13 teachers' guide stresses the use of methods related to a number of resource books intended to provide background information for teachers' use in planning their own science schemes. The Environmental Studies Project team also prepared a teachers' guide together with a number of case-studies exemplifying good practice in schools. The idea of producing learning packs which teachers would simply put to use in their classes was of course inimical to this approach. The Middle Years of Schooling Project was concerned with equipping teachers to carry out their own curriculum development and produced papers and discussion documents to aid this. Art and Craft Education 8–13 produced tape/slide kits to promote teachers' discussion and subsequent planning. The one project which did adopt a learning packages approach was Breakthrough to Literacy, but here the development of a range of identifiable language skills which could be achieved through the use of particular equipment was aimed at.

These projects in various ways tried to develop teacher expertise and understanding and, mainly because of this, it is impossible to state whether or how far they have influenced practice. This very concentration on teachers rather than materials respects autonomy and judgement with teachers arriving at a large number of curriculum solutions derived from the one source, according to how they perceive the curricular needs of their children. Short of surveying a vast number of classes and schools it is impossible to say how direct or pervasive the impact has been, except through research studies like ORACLE where the curriculum was more a side issue compared with the main intention of researching teacher styles. The projects themselves had limited durations and budgets. As dissemination takes place over a long period of time, the usual life span of three or four years is not enough to estimate the impact of a project on schools. It is significant that Geography for the Young School Leaver, the most successful Schools Council project judged by take-up, was funded for twice this amount of time and the team was conscious of the need to disseminate from the beginning. Likewise, Science 5–13 has been extended by a number of back-up projects aimed at increasing teachers' scientific knowledge and expertise and these are contributing to its adoption. Generally, how far the methods and materials of a project are adopted will depend on the quality of in-service provision in terms of how well it meets teachers' needs in relation to the project's requirements. All of the more recent Schools Council projects have recognized the need for in-service work as the main means by which the innovation reaches teachers beyond the trial schools. A major condition for implementation inheres in the child-centred and resource-based model of teaching and learning which most of the primary projects present. As the ORACLE research shows, there are a number of disparate teaching styles in primary schools, not all of which are child-centred, so the match between project philosophy and teacher style will not be precise in all cases. It is possible, for example, to find Science 5–13 materials being used as part of the syllabus in formally organized classrooms with teachers performing experiments in front of the class for the children to observe and record. Perhaps a major weakness is their house style; it is hard to see how the primary curriculum might be rethought or redefined through them if implicit in them is a model of teaching style and classroom organization which is a reification of the Plowden primary teacher.

The DES Survey: Primary Education in England

If Plowden was important as the apotheosis of child-centredness, the DES survey is equally so as a document which takes stock of the post-Plowden advances. What is most notable about it is its curriculum orientation. Dearden (1980) has pointed out its unPlowdenlike stance especially on the curriculum, and whereas Plowden was broad-based and concerned with relating theory to practice in developing a rationale for primary education, the survey is deliberately limited in scope. It was concerned with the 7–11 years junior school age group; five hundred and forty-two schools and over a thousand classes were surveyed through direct observation, testing and administering questionnaires to heads and teachers. It was complemented by a smaller survey published in 1982, *Education 5 to 9*, which is an examination of eighty infant and first schools.

The curriculum is discussed in three chapters and thus occupies a large part of the report. Chapter 5, on the content of the curriculum, may be seen as implicitly defining the nature and scope of the primary curriculum. Its list comprises language and literacy, which includes listening and talking, reading and writing; mathematics; science; aesthetic and physical education; and social studies, which includes religious education, history and geography. Social and moral learning is included with the point that they arise from the ethos of the school rather than being subjects. What is clearly evident in the report, as it was in the ORACLE findings, is that teachers spend a considerable amount of time on language and literacy and mathematics:

On the evidence of this survey, teachers in primary schools work hard to ensure that children master the basic techniques of reading and writing. There is little support for any view which considers that these aspects of language are neglected in primary schools. In the vast majority of classes, reading schemes and courses were used to provide children with material at the right level of difficulty and were used regularly. *(ref. 5.46, p. 51)*

Similarly with mathematics:

The findings of this survey do not support the view which is sometimes expressed that primary schools neglect the practice of the basic skills in arithmetic. In the classes inspected considerable attention was paid to computation, measurement and calculations involving sums of money, though the results of these efforts were disappointing in some respects. *(ref. 5.50, pp. 52-3)*

The most general criticism of teachers is that they did not stretch the more able children sufficiently and that the work in mathematics was over-mechanical. The inspectors perceived an entrenched traditional view in the teaching of basic skills. In language the emphasis was heavily on reading though teachers thought all aspects were important; in mathematics there was a strong computation bias. Mathematics also was seen in a narrow context with little connection being made to science through concepts such as weight, volume, velocity or speed and in only about a fifth of the classes were there any connections being made between mathematics and other curriculum activities. There was very little science teaching and what there was tended to be nature study. About two thirds of the classes had a nature or interest table and about half kept small animals. The report compares the effort put into developing science teaching in primary schools with the effects this has had:

During the past few years considerable efforts have been made to stimulate and support science teaching in primary schools. There have been curriculum development projects at national level and in some areas local authority advisors and teachers' centres have been very active. Guidance about the kind of science which is suitable for young children, its place in the curriculum and teaching methods is readily available in the publications of the Schools Council, the Nuffield Foundation, the Department of Education and Science and elsewhere. Yet the progress of science teaching in primary schools has been disappointing; the ideas and materials produced by curriculum development projects have had little impact in the majority of schools. *(ref. 5.82, p. 62)*

Art and craft were found to be well taught and links were made between this and mathematics through pictorial representation. Music too was taught satisfactorily. Physical education and music were the two activities most likely to be taught by specialist teachers throughout a school. The report was critical of the Christian bias in religious education in virtually all schools; the fact of a multi-faith society, it was suggested, has scarcely seemed to have influenced either teaching or the content of assemblies. While history and geography were treated separately it was recognized in the survey that they were often taught as contributors to a theme or project; history teaching generally was thought to be superficial and in many cases involved children in copying out material from reference books. There was little evidence of planning and few schools had schemes or guidelines for history. Geography, where it was expressed in studies of the locality, was successful and meaningful to the children. The report took a non-partisan view of project work: it is not the definitive way of treating topics in social studies but if well planned it can be effective:

Where history was taught through topics of general interest there was the danger of a fragmented approach. A framework is required to provide some ordering of the content being taught. This may be a single path through a chronological sequence or a more complex series of historical topics which, while not necessarily taught in chronological order, should give a perspective in terms of the ordering of events or by means of comparison with the present day. *(ref. 5.128, p. 73)*

What emerges from this brief account is curriculum fragmentation; of separate and arbitrary subjects being taught compared with the desirability of integrating the curriculum argued for in Plowden. In the ORACLE research it was noted that the group instructors were more likely than other teacher types to merge subject boundaries in their planning and that they were in the minority. What is clear is that for many teachers, basic skills understanding is paramount and to be secured and the rest of the curriculum is subservient to this. The official attitude to the curriculum is clear in the survey:

Curricular content should be selected not only to suit the interests and abilities of the children and to provide for the progressive development of the basic skills, but also because it is important in its own right. (ref. 8.25, p. 113)

There was resistance to any suggestion that if the curriculum was narrowed teachers would be better able to deal with it. The findings concluded that basic skills were best learned when they were

applied in other subjects. Also the view was that 'taking primary
schools as a whole, the curriculum is probably wide enough to serve
current educational needs'. *(p. 126)*

There appears to be an impasse between the integrationist
'seamless robe' thinking of Plowden and the commonsense theories
of knowledge held by teachers, perhaps for the instrumental reason
that the generalist nature of primary teaching entails that the class
teacher is responsible for everything that is taught in the class and
that the whole enterprise becomes manageable if subjects are
compartmentalized. This is often revealed in the planning
documents which schools use, in the form of syllabuses, guidelines
and schemes, to develop whole-school policies.

The basic subjects and what might be called an agreed 'core' at
least on paper are clearly represented in Figure 7. What is
surprising is that 43 per cent of the schools had science guidelines yet
the Inspectorate found found very little evidence of science teaching.

Another aspect of whole-school curriculum planning is the range
and influence of scale post-holders who are responsible for aspects
of the curriculum in a school. The distribution of these is
interesting: 70 per cent of schools had post-holders for music, and

Subject	% of schools	Subject	% of schools	Subject	% of schools
Mathematics	88	Music	37	Social studies	18
Language	85	History	36	Dance	17
Religious education	72	Geography	35	Health education	17
Science	43	Environmental studies	34	French	15
Art	42	Games	26	Humanities	9
Craft	41	Swimming	19	Other subjects	17
Gymnastics	38	Drama	18		

(*Primary Education in England*, p. 40)

Figure 7   *The percentage of schools with written guidelines or
schemes of work for each subject*

the next highest was for games, swimming and gymnastics, taken together. These two activities were most likely to be taught by specialists. About half the schools had language post-holders and rather fewer than half for mathematics. About a third had art and craft post-holders but only a fifth for science. The important question is, how effective were the post-holders as curriculum leaders in their schools? It might be expected that they would have a major say in policy making and especially in devising guidelines and schemes for the whole school. There were schemes, as the evidence shows, but only in about a quarter of the schools were there teachers with responsibility posts for aspects of the curriculum having what is described in the survey as 'considerable' influence on the quality of teaching and learning in their curricular areas. There was little evidence in most schools that such teachers exercised influence beyond their own classrooms. They were frequently examples of good practice but it was entirely up to their colleagues as to whether or not they learned from such examples. The reasons for this appear to lie partly with the dominant class-teacher system in schools and partly with the salary structure which supports a scale post system of advancement. The difficulties in bringing about curriculum change among teachers with considerable classroom autonomy have been discussed. So far as the salary structure is concerned, the way teachers are promoted in and between schools is through scale posts which give responsibility for some aspect of the school's life, be it music, school journeys or the library. Post-holders are increasingly seen as curriculum leaders but in many schools it has been the means by which effective staff can be rewarded. So there is a measure of role and responsibility invention inevitable in such a system; it is certainly a device whereby heads can retain enthusiastic young teachers who might otherwise look for promotion elsewhere. The survey comments that post-holders in curricular areas should be responsible for drawing up schemes of work, giving guidance to colleagues and for resourcing their aspect of the curriculum in schools. It is also important that they keep up to date with current thinking and practice.

Implementing change

The possibilities of in-school curriculum development draw attention to the potential role of post-holders and also advisory teachers, consultants and other curriculum specialists outside the school. It raises issues such as the efficacy of the change-agent role, the conditions for successful school-based development and the ways in which the hidden curriculum in a school or classroom both underpins and subverts the actual curriculum.

All curriculum leaders in schools are potential change agents, and some, such as consultants, overtly practice this. Hoyle (1971) believes that innovation is now a permanent aspect of educational practice, though he was writing at a time when the Schools Council projects were a significant part of the educational scene. He suggests that change moves from an unplanned to a planned stage through the founding of curriculum development agencies such as the Schools Council as the effects of the wave of curriculum development are felt in schools. As argued earlier here, the Schools Council's projects have, at best, brought about change which is difficult to quantify, and, at worst, hardly made an impression on the status quo curriculum. Since the demise of virtually all of the large-scale attempts to innovate, the notion of planned change has become a matter of local authority curriculum guidelines being drawn up as a response to pressure from central government for more control and accountability within the education system. At present, these have an advisory status, with schools being urged to take account of them when developing their own plans, but advisors and consultants are increasingly seen as promulgators of local authorities' considered views on aspects of the curriculum. In these conditions there is more curriculum change going on in schools than during the era of the Schools Council.

But there is still the possibility of tissue rejection, in Hoyle's terms, given teachers' freedom; if it is to be avoided, teachers and others must consider what are the best means of implementing change. The ways in which innovations are introduced are likely to determine the form and the degree of adoption; these strategies range from the authoritarian, where change is imposed on a staff by a head teacher, to the rational, where staff are consulted as professionals. Hoyle claims, along with Miles, that the school is the appropriate unit for change and that the group rather than the individual is the agent of change. He further suggests that schools might need the help of change agents.

The role of the change agent is fraught with difficulties in the delicate business of getting fellow professionals to review and possibly change their practices by adopting innovations. The relationship between an agent and a school needs to be voluntary and collaborative. More crucially, power between the head, staff and the agent should be equalized. There have been doubts about the change-agent role in education because it is a concept co-opted from industry where different conditions, values and ground rules apply. A chief problem is that while it is straightforward enough to analyse the practices in a factory or on a production line in order to recommend improvements, the complexities of schools and teachers make change agency a far from straightforward task.

The change agent in Hoyle's thinking would bring the theory behind the practice to the staff's attention, then analyse with the staff ways in which the innovation might be implemented. He would also remain to evaluate and to support the introduction of the change. But in the end the innovation will fail unless the staff believe in it:

An innovation foisted upon a school staff against its wishes is unlikely to lead to an improvement upon existing practice. Resistance to change is legitimate; one would be foolish to believe that all proposed change in education was for the better and the experience and commonsense of a school staff will often lead them to resist a change which they regard merely as a gimmick and making no improvement upon existing practice. *(Hoyle 1971, p. 73)*

The change agent must allow staff to work off their untenable objections and risk the possibility that this will not happen; at the same time, he must not over-identify with the proposed change since this will incur distrust.

An example of relatively successful change agency is the system of primary mathematics consultant teachers implemented fairly recently by the Inner London Education Authority. The consultants are drawn from experienced teachers who usually have been mathematics post-holders in primary schools for a number of years and have both undergone and organized in-service courses at teacher's centres. This record of successful experience and of in-service teacher education involvement is important to their credibility in schools. The scheme is financed through the Alternative Use of Resources (AUR) money scheme which is unique to the ILEA. Under this system, schools can supplement their resources either by buying materials and equipment or engaging extra part-time staff. A school chooses to 'buy' a mathematics consultant for one day per week for a school year but on the understanding that the 'purchase' will normally be for two years, since this is a feasible amount of time for the consultant to develop the mathematics teaching in the school. This is done through working with teachers usually selected by the head who can be expected to profit from the expertise and experience offered by the consultant. He/she has no routine duties in school and is there specifically to resource mathematics teaching. A consultant will work in four schools per week for one day each and spends the fifth day at a mathematics teachers' centre for personal in-service education aimed at extending and deepening expertise and understanding. The in-service time does not appear to be spent in considering the role itself of mathematics consultant or indeed the processes of implementing innovation through change agency. As the scheme has been operating for less than five years it is hard to judge its long-term success in raising the level of mathematics teaching in participating schools but forms of evaluation are being applied which should begin to reveal its effectiveness. Certainly, the change-agent conditions, as Hoyle states them, apply: he or she is in a school at the request of the staff, or at least the head teacher; the relationship is collaborative in that expertise is transmitted and shared. Power, however, is not equalized, and, given the amount of autonomy of heads in their own schools, it is hard to see how this could be brought about. But the change-agent process is rational in that it seeks to improve what is already there by involving teachers in rethinking what they do rather than trying to sell them new practices.

What of the potential change-agency role of post-holders as curriculum leaders? Considering what has been argued, it is hard to see how they might influence colleagues, given their official status and authority, unless they are particularly persuasive or charismatic. Possibly their influence could be strengthened from outside the school, in terms of the more systematic overseeing of the curriculum that all local authorities are obliged to operate, after the DES circular 14/77, *LEA Arrangements for the School Curriculum*. This required local authorities to submit a detailed account of how each was guiding and controlling the curriculum in schools, according to the responsibilities laid on them by the 1944 Education Act. At the school level this is often a matter of formulating guidelines for all or most curricular areas by bringing together people such as experienced teachers, inspectors, advisory teachers and academics. What is produced is advisory rather than obligatory, since, as suggested earlier their status is blurred, but the guidelines are a means by which schools can develop their own programmes of curriculum appraisal and possible renewal. The danger of course is that once a school staff can demonstrate this sort of evidence that it has thought about the school's curriculum, the schemes and guidelines can become enshrined in the school's daily work and seen as definitive. But they are also very much the basis for the sort of school-based development which Skilbeck has argued for and which the James Committee recommended. Eggleston (1980) traces this recent emphasis on school-based development to the Schools Council Working Paper 53, *The Whole Curriculum 13–16* (1975), which drew several threads together: the consolidation stages of large-scale curriculum development, resource-based learning as a response to mixed ability organization and individualized learning, and the James idea of school-based in-service training. He comments that although school-based development is widespread, it is by no means common; 'readiness' for such a development is important, such as when a school staff come to realize that there is a need for change in some aspect of their curriculum.

Skilbeck (1972) sees curriculum change as an aspect of cultural change. A recent illustration of this viewpoint is that due to the influence of the new technology, schools as users and creators of resources are being challenged in terms of how effectively they are responding to such social change. The key questions for Skilbeck are; is the school any longer the most effective institution in society for educating the young? Is the curriculum

performing the educative and other socially desirable functions
which are expected of it? He also notes some problems which are
likely to be encountered when teachers are involved in change.
Some are structural such as inadequate resources and rapid
turnover of staff, while others concern morale qualities of teachers
such as self-concepts, inadequacies in curriculum planning skills
and lack of interest and conviction.

The hidden curriculum

What is involved in any change process are the ways in which the
hidden curriculum in a school can both support and undermine the
actual curriculum. It has everything to do with teachers not only
being able to see the need for change but being able to accept likely
answers. Jackson (1968) first drew attention to what he described as
the 'hidden' curriculum:

which each student (and teacher) must master if he is to make his way
satisfactorily through the school. The demands created by these features of
classroom life may be contrasted with the academic demands – the 'official'
curriculum, so to speak – to which educators have traditionally paid most
attention. *(pp. 33-4)*

Jackson maintains that pupils' personal survival and success
depends on their understanding and conforming to the requirements
of the hidden curriculum of school and classroom and that teachers
also are intimately bound up in the relationship between the hidden
and the official or actual curriculum. For pupils it has a number of
characteristics which include learning to live in crowds, which
might imply postponing asking teachers for help when they are
dealing with others, sharing scarce resources, acquiring the ability
to tolerate disturbance, ambiguity and interruption, having the
capacity to wait to use materials and equipment that others are
using, having the ability to lose time and tolerate boredom and
passivity. Jackson comments that 'the quintessence of virtue in
most institutions is contained in the single word: patience'. As well
as all these, pupils must learn to accept assessment by their peers
and teachers, to learn to compete to please both peers and teachers

in order to win praise, to learn how to live in a hierarchical society and to be differentiated in the process.

Much of this involves learning how to control teachers by controlling the pace of learning through using diversionary tactics. The five-year-old in a reception class who requires to go to the toilet when faced with an unwanted task, and the fifteen-year-old who has perfected the art of asking diversionary questions to get a teacher on to a favourite hobby horse are aiming at the same goal. Shared meanings are learned quickly as being the means by which individuals keep afloat in highly structured face-to-face environments. Children in fact learn what schools are before they actually go to school by playing 'school'. Eggleston cites the case of his 3-year-old son who while looking at some promotional literature from a mail-order book firm on a new edition of Churchill's war memoirs, exclaimed 'Daddy, it's a headmaster!' on seeing a photograph of Churchill in typically belligerent mood. The young child has much to learn as quickly as possible, as Eggleston (1977) comments:

For the new pupil arriving in an established class, the learning of the hidden curriculum becomes an urgent necessity, preceding any hope of effective participation in the official curriculum. Where shall he sit and how? What fine balance of attention or indifference is tolerable both to the teacher and to his classmates? How fully can he respond to the teacher's questioning? With what vocabulary and what intonation may he talk to the teacher? What are the expectations of the teacher concerning talking in class, performance of written work, honesty of marking? Which of his fellow pupils and teachers must he learn to respect and tolerate; which must he learn to distrust and not tolerate? *(pp. 113-14)*

The teacher is also of course subject to the norms and conditions of the hidden curriculum. The nature of the teacher education course, as the agency of professional socialization by which new teachers are inducted into teaching, will influence at the beginning of their careers how they evaluate teaching situations and how they account for their own practices. Their first teaching post will modify their initial analyses, sometimes drastically. Important here are the way teachers perceive children as learners in an educative process within which there are certain received views, some in accord, some conflicting, on the nature of learning and teaching. For example,

Sharp and Green (1975) have considered the vocabulary of accounting in their study of a primary school whose staff favoured child-centred approaches. Their transcribed interviews with teachers reveal conflicts between adherence to child-centred teaching methods and what the teachers perceived to be children's limitations, due to their supposedly culturally impoverished home backgrounds. The vocabulary available to teachers is inadequate for them to deal with their curriculum practices; terms such as 'readiness', 'stage' and 'needs' have a textbook value which does not encompass classroom realities when they try to explain these. This problem raises the general point about the applicability of theoretical models and is important for the larger issue of teachers rejecting educational theory as having little connection with practice.

Meighan (1981) has described the classroom as 'haunted' – by the architect who designed it and by book writers, resource designers and materials producers all of whom stamp their own beliefs, prejudices and preconceptions of schooling on the inhabitants. It is haunted also by those who developed language usage and in particular the dichotomies which mark English: black/white, good/bad, strong/weak and so on. The cumulative effect that these factors have on teachers is that normally they are threatened by the prospect of change and will strive to maintain the status quo as being the model of equilibrium they have achieved in their day-to-day practices. Change requires a redefinition of curriculum knowledge which challenges the cultural schema which support it. One case of strong feelings being generated both for and against the product was Leila Berg's Nippers series of primary readers. Where traditional reading schemes expressed middle-class values through the families they portrayed – two children, a housewife mother and a father who goes to work wearing a suit and carrying a briefcase – these expressed working-class life in a humorous and naturalistic manner. Some head teachers welcomed them, others refused to have them in their schools because, ostensibly, they ran counter to the school culture: fathers were sometimes reluctant to get out of bed and go to work, families had fish and chip suppers as a treat, and there was a rather shady car-dealer uncle.

Meighan's analysis of school subjects reveals that school knowledge is not neutral and that redefinition of it through curriculum development will convey one view rather than another. Thus, the project team for Science 5–13 were at pains to delimit the notion of science which was not presented as a hard-edged, rigorous subject but as something which children come to study through their natural explorations. In this way they sought to reassure primary teachers who perhaps lacked scientific understanding; ironically, the project did not take at first because teachers did not believe that they had sufficient understanding of science to be able to operate it.

The conditions of school-based development

A case-study of change in a school will be illustrative in what school-based curriculum development entails for teachers in terms of recognizing the demands of the hidden and the actual curriculum and of teachers' attitudes to change. Forward (1976), a junior school head, discusses the changes which were brought about in his school through a reconsideration of its aims, curriculum and organization. This process began with a briefing through staff discussions and papers under the leadership of the head who had returned from being a Teacher Fellow at a university institute of education. The staff began a detailed analysis of the school's curriculum and a number of sub-divisions or headings were agreed. These were: the intellectual or academic area, the physical area, the personal and social development area and the aesthetic area. They tried to determine their relative importance by giving them ratings on a star system. Oracy and literacy emerged as the most important, with numeracy and mathematics next. The rest of the curriculum they described as 'general studies', and, in this, their curricular views were in broad agreement with the ORACLE research and the DES survey's findings.

They identified a number of skills such as the ability to follow instructions, classify materials and use audio visual and library resources. The aesthetic area which had been rated highly before the exercise began was reaffirmed during this period of appraisal and principles building. Personal and social development was thought to have been underemphasized in the past. As these major procedural questions were answered, further questions about the means of achieving them emerged, and it was clear that the curriculum and organization of the school would need much alteration. The staff took the first goal to be that of individualizing children's work as far as possible which argued a need for flexible grouping. This further entailed that the staff work more as a team and that as individuals they would relinquish in part their traditional classroom autonomy.

The staff began to develop a style of limited team teaching based on the co-operative teaching pattern already in the school. Team suites were established in which three or four teachers operated by pooling their strengths and skills. There were team co-ordinators, but no team leaders; this was decided by the head after having seen team teaching operating in other schools. Each team member had equal responsibility for planning and running the unit. Suites of rooms were planned, for groups of approximately eighty children, by rearranging class-rooms and modifying cloakrooms in what was a conventional class-teacher designed school. No major outlay from the local authority was needed but the advisors' help was valued. It was recognized that the children would need to be trained in the use of the team suites and this began to result in their being more independent of teachers and also more careful with materials and equipment than they had been before.

Forward observes that there were four stages in the development of the new organization: first, doubts and reservations, followed by acceptance and then enthusiasm, with the fourth stage being reflexive in nature as the staff's self-assessments were converted into data for improving the organization. What was crucial to success was the high level of staff commitment, and he feels that this was due to everyone being involved in the decision-making. At the time of writing, Forward reports that the new organization had settled down, curricular needs were being developed further and they were moving towards achieving their original aims.

This is a good example of Skilbeck's rational interactive model of curriculum decision-making, where teachers work as a group in defining through analysis what their situation requires in terms of curriculum change, and then deciding on and implementing innovation. What is important is that the staff were concerned with the whole situation of the school and that this enabled them to conceptualize what they perceived to be the desired changes rather than to accept what was successful and established and adjust this to suit a modified range of objectives. It is this whole-school approach which is so important to school-based change. An innovation in an area of the curriculum is likely to disturb or affect the whole, and to develop one or two aspects in insolation to the whole is to invite imbalance and further problems concerning the range of skills needed by teachers and children to operate with the new order. A new approach to mathematics teaching, for example, will affect those curricular areas in which mathematics is used, such as science and project work, because of the new perceptions about the nature of primary mathematics it is likely to engender. A school curriculum is organic and not simply a collection of syllabuses, schemes and guidelines which teachers utilize. Because of this it is important that both the organizational and the more pervasive influences affecting change are identified clearly and incorporated into the newly evolving curriculum. These influences include the development to multi-cultural curricula from those which are ethnocentric, the changes needed to meet the learning requirements of handicapped children in ordinary schools, the problem of differential achievement of boys and girls in some aspects of the curriculum, and the overarching issue of the new technology in schools, which will be considered in the next chapter.

Summary

Primary curriculum thought and practice has possibly reached a point where substantive questions have been settled, in contrast to the secondary curriculum where major issues are still being raised about its balance, coverage and relevance. This situation is revealed in official documents and in recent research studies such as ORACLE. The Schools Council's early work in primary education constituted piecemeal development in curricular areas where the most emphasis was needed, such as science; later development encompassed virtually the whole of the curriculum, but the Middle Years of Schooling Project was the only one to adopt a holistic viewpoint. The Schools Council's study of the nature of projects suggests both internal and external shaping influences on development. The primary projects tend to exemplify internal, school and teacher focused influences in that they concentrate on method rather than content. The presentation of projects to teachers is often through good examples of practice. Because primary projects have tried to develop teacher expertise and understanding with this emphasis, it is difficult to state whether or how far they have improved practice in schools. To compound this, there is the possibility of curriculum materials being used by teachers in a way which disassociates them from the original project, such as Science 5–13 materials being used didactically.

The DES primary and first school surveys are important as documents which take stock of post-Plowden developments. What is notable is their curriculum orientation. The core of the main survey consists of a detailed discussion of the primary curriculum in which the parameters for what can be seen as an official core or common curriculum can be discerned. It is evident from the survey that teachers spend a good deal of time on language and mathematics. A disappointing aspect was the dearth of effective science teaching, but, more fundamentally, the survey revealed possible curriculum fragmentation through teachers taking a strongly subjects-based view of the curriculum and because of the superficiality of much project and topic work. Another important factor for whole-school planning was the lack of influence as curriculum leaders of many post-holders. It is to be expected that they would have responsibilities for producing schemes and guidelines, probably based on the local authority schemes, for the school in their curricular areas but in practice the majority had little or no influence in their schools.

This draws attention to the potential of the change-agent role and the conditions in which change agents need to operate if they are to be successful. The ILEA primary mathematics consultants scheme is a good example of classical change agency in an educational context.

Skilbeck raises a number of questions about the school's ability to respond to social change and the implications these have for teachers. But the context of curriculum change is formed by the ways the hidden curriculum influences the actual curriculum, and the roles of post-holders, heads and teachers in the change process have to be seen in terms of this interaction. Teachers' and pupils' roles are structured by the workings of the hidden curriculum, which is the network of norms, mores and covertly acceptable practices which underpin and virtually decide all that is taught and learned. Children learn what it is to be pupils in their reception classes, and their school careers in terms of this role are elaborated and refined with each year at school. Also, teachers' own perceptions of what it is to be a teacher are shaped by the interactions of the hidden with the actual curriculum. The curriculum change implications are that teachers will tend to maintain their status quo as being the model of equilibrium they have achieved in their daily work. Change requires a redefinition of curriculum knowledge which inevitably challenges the cultural schema which supports the curriculum.

The example of whole-school development given here illustrates the position of the head teacher as the most influential figure in a primary school. The change process is rational and ordered, beginning with an appraisal of the present state of the school and a restatement of the desired curricular and organizational changes carried out by the head and his staff working as a group.

Further reading

Department of Education and Science (1978), *Primary Education England: A Survey by HM Inspectors of Schools*, London: HMSO

Department of Education and Science (1982), *Education 5-9: an illustrative Survey of 80 First Schools in England*, London: HMSO

Meighan, R. (1981), *A Sociology of Educating*, Eastbourne: Holt, Rinehart and Winston
    Part 2 is a detailed analysis of the workings of the hidden curriculum.

6. Curriculum issues in primary education

The nature of the issues

There remains much to be done to the primary curriculum to accommodate and adapt practice to a number of issues such as the integration of children with special educational needs into ordinary schools, the development of curricula which more closely represent the multicultural nature of this society, the fact of gender stereotyping and differential achievement of boys and girls which is confirmed by the time they reach the secondary school, and the impact of new technology on schools. These are the issues which teachers can work directly with; more pervasive is the issue of curriculum commonality raised for the first time by central government in 1977 through the 'Red Book', *Curriculum 11-16*, and developed in discussion and policy-making papers produced by the Inspectorate and the DES. The later ones are concerned not only with the secondary curriculum and its problems but also with laying down possible guidelines for the whole curriculum for the statutory age range of 5–16 years. With the drive towards commonality, the issue of the technician-teacher is raised, operating according to performance objectives set by local authorities responding to central directives. If curriculum commonality is one side of the coin, then standards of achievement, and the accountability on the part of teachers for attaining certain results in children's learning, is the other side. The establishment of the Assessment of Performance Unit in 1974 with its ambitious programme of monitoring pupil attainment across the primary and secondary curriculum has been noted in the Introduction. Although its work has been scaled down, the data obtained could readily be transformed into norms for teachers to achieve, given certain political climates, as Lawton (1980) has pointed out.

The direction of these issues is towards teachers appraising their work and making explicit the values that guide their practice. For issues such as the treatment of children with special needs and the development of curricula which satisfies the policy of equal opportunity and recognizes cultural diversity, there are no clear guidelines and a wealth of conflicting value positions. Little has been attempted by way of curriculum development except for the Schools Council project 'Education for a Multicultural Society'; all three issues have generated polemic, and little is known in substance about teachers' attitudes to them.

Special educational needs

So far as children with special educational needs are concerned, the policy situation at central government and local authority levels is clear. The Warnock Report in 1978 established four interrelated areas which the committee saw as most needing attention: provision for children under 5 with special educational needs, to include recognizing the role of parents as their children's first educators; the expansion of nursery education for all children and the provision of a range of specialist help; provision for young people over 16 with special needs to include more and better opportunities to continue their education at school or in further education and to receive career guidance; and the inclusion in teacher education courses of a special education element and increased in-service training for qualified teachers. Implicit in all these is the general principle of integrating children with special needs into ordinary schools which the majority of local authorities are carrying out. The 1981 Education Act (Special Educational Needs) established the right for these children to have an education which takes into account their learning difficulties. It is the duty of the local authority to identify and assess children over the age of 2 and to make suitable provision for them both in ordinary and special schools. The Act, according to its critics (for instance see Brennan, 1982), does not meet the Warnock recommendations but it does at least reinforce the rights of these children to a complete education.

The issue of integration and its implications have been explored through a three-year research study carried out by the NFER and funded by the DES (Hegarty, Pocklington and Lucas, 1981). They acknowledge that integration has become a slogan word with the practical implications yet to be worked out. They consider Warnock's three suggested forms of integration: locational, where there are special units or classes set up in ordinary schools or where a special and an ordinary school share the same site; social, where children attending a special unit mix with other children socially; and functional, which is the fullest form of integration where children with special needs work alongside ordinary children full-time or part-time and are in every sense members of the school's community. The researchers identify a number of difficulties with the notion of integration which have to do with its acquired slogan status, its different meanings and the misconceptions about the nature of special educational treatment in relation to integration. The study offers a number of curriculum case studies of effective practice from which the researchers conclude that two principles, 'normalization' and special action to meet special needs, were central. But in the majority of cases surveyed, teachers operated between these two in trying to organize the mainstream curriculum for ordinary children and those with special needs alike but making particular provisions for the handicapped children. The researchers acknowledge that curriculum disputes in mainstream education are matched by those in special education; they see these as essentially being disputes over basing the curriculum on some conception of life skills, or on conventional subjects or disciplines. The curriculum for slow learners with whatever handicap has been marked by an over-emphasis on the basics to the detriment of other activities, or it has been a watered-down version of the mainstream curriculum. More recently there has been an emphasis on teachers planning by behavioural objectives which concentrate on those classroom factors which teachers can control; it is a rigorous application of the rational curriculum planning model:

The approach rests on defining teaching goals, breaking them down into precisely stated and carefully sequenced behavioural objectives, and monitoring pupils' progress through continuous systematic assessment. *(Hegarty,* et al. *1981, p. 322)*

The researchers offer a tentative outline of provision based on a continuum which moves from special curriculum to normal curriculum. This then ranges from a curriculum which is based on self help, socialization and oral communication through to a point where it is accepted that all children are educable, which, at the other end of the continuum, entails making adjustments to the mainstream curriculum to accommodate children with special needs. The form and extent of integration clearly depends on the nature and extent of the handicap. With ancillary help and positive teacher attitudes, physically handicapped children can be integrated successfully, particularly in infant and junior schools, but as the curriculum broadens and their peers outstrip them it will be increasingly hard for schools to develop full provisions. Again, the researchers offer case studies of successful integration, though many teachers in the study felt that they could not adequately meet needs in the ordinary classroom, or accurately assess the potential of handicapped children. All the case studies cry out for the kind of in-service training asked for by Warnock. Other factors of classroom life posed difficulties, such as how far to discipline children who had not yet learned how to behave in ordinary schools. Many expected the same level of individual attention which they had grown to expect in their special schools, and a vicious circle was set up, with teachers not being sure how they should deal with the children, and the children, faced with this uncertainty, not being placed in a position where they could learn how they should behave.

Meighan (1981) raises questions about the process of being labelled 'special' and its consequences. He questions both the effectiveness of the process and the instruments used to define special needs, which even if they were reliable would be defeated by the variations in different local authorities. The notion of screening is borrowed from medicine and like co-opted terms and ideas is not necessarily effective in its new location. He maintains that screening is premised on the assumption that a proportion of children, 20 per cent according to the Warnock Committee, are too 'ill' in educational terms for normal schooling; they have handicaps for which a range of treatment in special education is available according to the diagnosis and the local authority's policy of providing for special educational needs. He further argues that this social pathology approach does not include inquiring into possible causes of educational handicap such as school regimes, learning climates, teachers' expectations and prevailing ideologies of education: cause in this account lies entirely with the individual.

The social pathology view has several educational consequences. Teachers' expectations will vary and with these the performance of pupils. A 'therapeutic' notion of education might come to be practised by teachers in special schools, and perhaps by remedial teachers in ordinary schools, rather than the cognitively orientated notion which applies to normal children. Screening, too, will be imperfect and there will be incorrect diagnoses. Meighan cites an approach to educational failure used in Salford where the problems of slow learners were redefined as teachers' problems; as a result, where in 1969 about 25 per cent of seven-year-olds moving from the infant to the junior school were classified as non-readers, by 1978 this figure had dropped to 6 per cent. The strategy was based on breaking down the self-fulfilling prophecy by which slow learners were blamed for their apparent inability to learn.

It might be felt that integration as a policy should be upheld as an antidote to underlining the label of handicapped or slow learner. Certainly, the isolating effect that attending a special school can have, along with the stigma attaching to special education, can be lessened. The policy of screening and separation has more than a hint of the cost-effective and tidy-minded about it, since it is convenient to group children with similar learning handicaps to work with specially trained teachers. A more humane account suggests that such children will be failures in ordinary schools and by placing them in ordinary schools they are protected as being the most vulnerable of children. At a commonsense level it would seem that grossly handicapped children, mentally, emotionally and physically, might need special education, but where is the line to be drawn between those who need this and those who will gain from attending an ordinary school? The answers are likely to be as arbitrary as were eleven-plus results not so long ago, where the grammar and secondary-modern selection process operated in accordance with the proportion of places available in the different types of school as much as with individual children's performance in the tests. Also, it is significant that much of the discussion so far has perceived slow learners of whatever description as being problems; what about the high achievers, the gifted children? Perhaps because they are not seen as being problems, very little by way of special provisions are made for them by local authorities.

Ethnic differences and the curriculum

It is significant that the education of children from ethnic minority groups is likewise seen as being a problem since they do not easily fit into the mainstream of education unless they somehow cease to be different and become part of the mainstream culture. Briefly, the history of educational thinking and policy making began with the concept of assimilation: that the children of immigrant parents who might themselves be immigrants would be best served if they were as fully as possible assimilated into the culture of the host society. This entailed heavy emphasis on language programmes in primary schools to equip the children with Standard English, and ignoring their obvious differences compared with indigenous children in matters of religious beliefs and customs, diet and clothing. This view slowly gave way to the notion of integration whereby children from different cultures were mainly treated as if they had the same educational needs as indigenous children but had curious beliefs and customs in their out of school lives which needed to be accepted in school in the same way that individual differences were. Again, this shaded into a cultural pluralist stance which encompasses a number of positions. At one extreme there is token acceptance by teachers of children's cultural differences with a concentration on the more colourful manifestations of these. Perhaps less extreme is the genuine attempt to get to grips with cultural differences which results in Indian Evenings in schools, steel bands and an emphasis on costume, food, religion and ritual. The most positive stance is suggested by an acknowledgement and acceptance of cultural difference which recognizes that this is a multicultural society and that schools need to develop curricula which recognize cultural diversity.

It is true to say that versions of assimilationism, integrationism and cultural pluralism are to be found in schools today. It is not uncommon for primary teachers ostensibly to deny that, for instance, there are black, brown, white and yellow children in their classes: there are, simply, children, all of whom have the same learning needs and the right to equal, that is, the same, treatment. This can lead to a reinforcement of what still is a highly ethnocentric school curriculum with little more than token gestures made to multiculturalism in materials such as reading schemes, books and posters. What is problematic is that in some cases there will be genuine differences demanding particular skills and perhaps different educational treatment.

A major problem that Meighan suggests is that of terminology – 'immigrant' is still used by some to describe second and third generation children, especially of Afro-Carribean origin. 'Race' is meaningless in biological terms; defining people according to race or colour is a social rather than a biological description. With the labels come pecking orders; if children from ethnic minorities are seen as being problems to schools then it is a short step to perceiving them as culturally disadvantaged and therefore inferior to middle-class indigenous children. There is a growing research literature on the effects of such social and cultural labelling: they include conflicts of identity to the extent of denying the colour of one's skin, low self-esteem and induced low achievement. There is often the ambivalent attitudes of teachers. Pidgeon (1970) concluded from his research that a high proportion of teachers still held a 'capacity' view of the nature of intelligence many decades after this view had been successfully challenged; Goodacre's research referred to earlier demonstrated that many teachers had low expectations of working-class children's achievenments in the process of learning to read; Bernstein (1970) was at pains to lay the ghost of cultural deprivation attributed to him by those who misinterpreted his research especially on the nature of language codes. This earlier work on the cultural labelling of working-class children is directly comparable with the later research into the effects of labelling children from ethnic minorities. But there is a growing pressure to appraise: Stone (1981) as a result of her research denies the inevitability of the negative self-image among children of West Indian origin:

I suggest that an awareness of the historical role of black consciousness as shown in religious and political movements, in literature, poetry, music and song would lead researchers towards a better appreciation of black self-concept and self-image. Social scientists in Western society tend to operate in an ethnocentric trap where they (a) ignore black culture or (b) regard it as a pathological manifestation of white culture. . . The result of this is that even when in their own terms black children manifest positive self-concept and high self-esteem, social scientists explain it away either as the operation of an 'inflated mechanism' (Weinreich) or by reference to some other dubious 'theory'. *(p. 37)*

Jeffcoate (1979; 1981) explores the possibility of what he describes as a multiracial curriculum, for which there are at least four justifications which are based on what he calls a pathological foundation – the assumption that racism is a cultural norm in this society which inevitably colours children's views and images. Schools have a duty towards their children to counter this by encouraging racial self-respect and understanding; it is the task of schools to present to children an honest and accurate picture of the world as it is and a curriculum which is multiracial involves children in superior learning experiences than one which is ethnocentric. The counter views, he suggests, are that race is not important to children, that schools should transmit a British culture and that a multiracial curriculum will be unacceptably political in its orientation. What a multiracial or multicultural curriculum would look like for teachers and children is still a further question. Jeffcoate suggests criteria for the selection of learning experiences which take as their basis the denial that an ethnocentric curriculum can be justified in a multicultural society, the need to recognize the presence of different social and ethnic ·groups, the need for pupils to have access to accurate information about cultural differences and similarities, the need to portray individuals from ethnic groups in order to avoid stereotyping and the need to describe other countries in terms of their own values and practices and not against British norms.

But in practice the idea of a multiracial or multicultural curriculum is often associated with the ideology and practices of compensatory education. The notion that working-class children were 'culturally disadvantaged' implied that they needed to be compensated educationally for the deficiencies in their home background which made them under-achieve in school. The Plowden Committee claimed that this need to compensate children should be an important educational aim; Keddie and others (1971; 1973) pointed out that the problem was about cultural difference and not deficit. Merson and Campbell (1974) criticized the development as producing a down-town curriculum for down-town children, and Boyd (1977) related community education and attempts to develop community-based curricula to the dominant model of compensatory education. Stone comments:

There is an unexamined assumption that MRE (multiracial education) is a 'good thing' not dissimilar to the assumptions about progressive education in the early seventies. Any real concern about MRE has to face the problem that so far the only criticisms of it come from the right-wing which has encouraged a certain complacency and consensus among its practitioners. I want to suggest that MRE is conceptually unsound, that its theoretical and practical implications have not been worked out and that it represents a developing feature of urban education aimed at 'watering down' the curriculum and 'cooling out' black city children while at the same time creating for teachers, both radical and liberal, the illusion that they are doing something special for a particularly disadvantaged group. *(Stone 1981, p. 100)*

She argues that MRE is based on a social pathology view of ethnic minority children and suggests that its advocates believe that an education based on cultural differences will help children develop pride in their identity and group, encourage white children to view their black classmates more positively, reduce alienation and make schooling more relevant through new curricula which in turn will help provide better motivation and more positive attitudes to schools. Such aims are vague and being little more than sentiments, give little guidance for practice. What is happening in many local authorities, she claims, is a rejuvenation of the same spirit of positive discrimination which inspired the Plowden educational priority area projects. So, there tends to be an emphasis on language programmes and the development of materials in which the more general and visible ethnic and minority differences are recognized. Whether these types of measure will be productive is hard to say. There are no clear-cut answers, and perhaps it is the liberal, implicit racism of many teachers that prevents answers from being formulated. Right-wing racist views are unambiguous but when the Rampton Committee, composed of educationalists and others in sympathy with the needs and rights of children from a particular ethnic minority group, produced an interim report in 1981 entitled 'West Indian Children in Our Schools,' it can be seen how deeply rooted the ethnocentric conception of education is in Britain. Certainly, the initial task for teachers is to confront the possibility that their teaching is ethnocentric and that underlying their practices are racist views, whatever their own explicit moral, political and educational ideologies might be. Then perhaps the possibilities of a multicultural curriculum might be addressed by individual teachers with some chance of arriving at real answers to real educational needs, rather than seeing the children negatively as problems.

Gender and the curriculum

So far as gender issues in educational achievement are concerned, similar issues and lines of thinking apply. Again, preconceptions about the nature of difference are at the root of these. There has been and is the acceptance of different roles for men and for women picking out and reinforcing what were taken to be different innate characteristics. Children acquire their gender differentiation almost at birth through their names, and their early life is governed by what is seen by parents and others as appropriate behaviour, playthings and interests. Mothers and fathers treat their children differently, so that boys normally are expected to show aggressiveness and will, while girls are expected to behave with decorum and good humour.

Meighan claims that recognition of sex differences in education only became an official issue in 1973 when HMI were asked to undertake an inquiry into school curricula with reference to the possibly unequal opportunities it presented to girls and boys. Earlier, the longitudinal study carried out by Douglas (1964) suggested differential performances which affected life chances. Meighan considers the explanations offered for this: one psychological view suggests that girls inherit different aptitudes and abilities from boys and that differential curricula and treatment follows a 'natural' pattern. Another view suggests that girls inherit different personality traits and therefore schools, in providing for different motivations which have the consequences of producing different types of achievement, again are following a biologically determined law. Deem (1978) maintains that the influential research conducted by the Newsoms in the 1950s and 1960s was premised on a view that sex differences are innate, leading to different patterns of behaviour developing, so that when children choose activities, their choice is determined by whether they are boys or girls. Other researchers have drawn socially orientated conclusions for the same sort of work. The Newsoms observe that these activities are the same when the children are at home and in school. Seven-year-old girls were more likely to include reading and writing among their interests compared with boys of the same age; making models is mainly a boys' activity, while knitting and sewing were distinctively girls' activities. Both boys and girls play ball games but with boys this is more likely to be in a competing teams context such as football or cricket, while girls favour solitary rhythmic ball games. Dolls are a particularly significant means by which sex-role typing is learned and reinforced; for girls, dolls represent a means by which girls reinact and learn female behaviour while the Action Man type of boys' doll emphasizes masculine adventure. The Newsoms argue that girls' play mirrors the activities of adult women which are important to them, while boys' play depends more on fantasy, imagination and creativity since men's work is not visible to them.

It would be naive to suggest that these represent 'natural' activities though the Newsoms often sound as if this were so. The stamping in of behaviour which differentiates boys and girls is thorough and includes virtually all aspects of their lives. Inevitably it is reflected in the school curriculum, particularly at secondary level. But here, traditionally female subjects such as home economics are slowly being opened up for boys and male subjects like craft and design technology for girls under the momentum of equal opportunities legislation and the positive attitudes to equality that this is beginning to engender. Deem suggests:

Whilst boys appear to compensate for their relatively poorer reading performance and verbal skills by developing spatial, mechanical and analytic skills in the sciences and mathematics, girls seem frequently to capitalise on the verbal skills already acquired, without seriously attempting to develop or improve other skills. This helps to confine them to 'feminine' subjects and the arts. *(Deem 1978, p. 44)*

She also claims that sexism in learning is less apparent in primary compared with secondary schools because the range of subjects is smaller and the organization is geared more to individuals than class learning. She and others have pointed to one area, reading, in which sexist attitudes are commonly displayed through the portrayal of boys and girls in reading schemes:

women are often portrayed as playing passive roles, as princesses or 'damsels in distress', or are helped and advised in their exploits by men. Less important female characters are most often described in domestic roles, engaging in tasks like cooking, washing up, ironing or cleaning floors, while menfolk look on. Men and boys usually have a more interesting time, even if they are shown in a family context because they are able to go on outings, make models, take motor bikes and cars to pieces, never cook, wash up or clean, and are the only people who drive cars. *(Deem 1978, pp. 45-6)*

Similar things could be said about the class basis of reading materials with the emphasis being on the nuclear family which in most cases is also white.

The hidden curriculum aspects of sexism are possibly more influential: girls and boys lining up separately to come in from the playground or into assembly, girls doing most of the clearing up after art and craft work. The presence of a majority of women in primary schools may appear to present girls with suitable authority figures but primary teaching, especially with nursery and infant-aged children, has been thought of traditionally as a woman's job and low down on the status pecking order within the profession. Also the uncertain status of teaching as a minor profession further depresses status positions within it. There is research evidence (for example, see C. Lobban, 1978) suggesting that teachers are more likely to pay attention to the boys in a class because they are the noisier and the harder to control, or are expected to be, and also more demanding of attention. Deem suggests that a consequence of more attention being paid to the boys could be neglect of the girls so that early on in their schooling they do not develop the habit of asking questions about problems in their work because they are used to working with less help from the teacher. The remedy for this lies with the individual perceptions of teachers and their ability to modify what they see as being shortcomings in their teaching in the form of one-sided classroom interchanges.

The new technology and the primary curriculum

It is a truism that children are more at home with the new technology than their parents and often their teachers. The array of automated toys and electronic games have familiarized children with electronics, and toys such as Bigtrak and its computerized movements have introduced young children to the basics of programming as Holloway (1982) has commented:

Children of a very tender age are quite able to turn the TV on and off and to change choice of channels to suit individual tastes. Our youngest generation are 'button pushers' and 'switchers' from a very early age by the very design of children's toys. In every home, children gain experience of many patterns of behaviour, both natural and electronic. *(p. 59)*

Children are demonstrating that they are adept at complex and imaginative programming through the work of people such as Papert (1980) with his 'turtles', the number of young people who are making considerable amounts of money from selling their own computer games to manufacturers and the growing number of teachers who work with microprocessors in their classrooms.

What is clear is that as the early generations of microprocessors are developed and made even more readily available than they are at present, there will be major changes in social and practical living styles which schools will need to respond to through their curricula. A national survey conducted in 1980 revealed that only about thirty schools were using microprocessors but by 1981 the number, judging from conferences and courses attendance, had risen to several hundred. This is very much in accord with the very rapid and continuing development and availability of micro-processors. Also, the government has demonstrated its full commitment to their use in schools through its Microelectronics in Education Programme (MEP). What is becoming clear with use is that microprocessors as the main manifestation of the new technology have application across the curriculum. Dodridge (1982) suggests that areas such as the humanities, geography and history need to call upon large data-bases of information which could extend the normal resources provided by a school library. Aspects of mathematics such as sorting into sets, studying the properties of shapes and using bar graphs and histograms for example are suitable for computer work, as are number fractions, place value and number bases in arithmetic. Dodridge also suggests that science through the study of electronics, history and geography through map work and diagrams, and music making could be enhanced through the use of computers.

What is crucial is that teachers become skilled in working with computers to the extent that they can program them or be able to critically evaluate programs and the variety of equipment on the market. Only then will they begin to integrate computers into their classrooms in such a way that they inform the whole curriculum. With infant-aged children, Holloway has described the main need as 'pre-computer skills'. She suggests that wiring puppets for sound and connecting them to cassette recorders on which instructions have been recorded will help children to work with more complex and impersonal electronic aids such as Language Masters, tape recorders and language laboratories. Children should then be introduced to projected light through an overhead projector so that they will be able to help produce basic audio visual material such as taped commentaries for stories illustrated on overhead projector transparencies. Keyboard skills are needed to use computers and these can be acquired by children by using large type-face or jumbo typewriters which will also accept projector transparencies. At this point children can be introduced to microprocessors using simple and well-proven programs which can be linked to display material in the classroom. She suggests that:

> Computers and infant-aged children appear to have common elements. Primarily, both will only accept input with the criteria of their unique known experience (in the case of the microcomputer, a known language; and in the case of the child, at a language level suitable to his perceptual and conceptual development). Secondly, instructions must be in suitable, logical steps because neither children nor computers can anticipate the instructions to follow nor can they correct ambiguous or misleading commands. *(Holloway 1982, p. 64)*

Activities such as early mathematics and early reading and writing skills are very suitable to computer usage, but the general aim will be to accustom children to the developed form of individualized learning offered by computers and to equip them with the necessary keyboard skills.

The main problem in the acceptance of microprocessors in classrooms is teachers' conservatism and fear; the first accompanies all aspects of educational change as has been discussed. The second derives from the advance and decline of the programmed learning movement in the 1960s when teachers genuinely feared that the 'teaching machines' rather than being classroom aids to learning, could actually reduce teachers' roles and even eventually supplant teachers. Microprocessors will be regarded in this light until teachers realize that it is the program, and not the machine, which is the crucial element, and that teachers are in a good position to ally themselves with programmers who will be able to draw upon teachers' professional expertise and experience in profitable collaboration. What is clear is that the sheer ubiquity of electronic aids will ensure that they will be adopted. What is less certain is that their high potential will be realized. There is the danger that they might be used merely as a source of amusement in spare moments or only in mathematics teaching.

Golby (1982) is concerned with what he calls the new technological tradition developing in primary schools which he contrasts with the more familiar elementary and developmental ideologies. He dates the beginning of this trend to the Great Debate in which there was a re-emphasis on the possibility of technology being the means to social progress. In the DES primary survey, science was taken to be part of an implicitly agreed primary core curriculum which signifies the importance of technology as applied science. A major problem which the survey highlighted was the tendency for the small amount of science teaching which the Inspectorate witnessed to take the form of natural rather than physical science, finding its expression in nature and interest tables in classrooms. What Golby envisages is a rethought social studies curriculum responding to the major social changes brought about by the new technology, and having the aim of helping children to understand the importance and potential of the new technology at work. In this way, microprocessors will be taken as problematic influences rather than teaching aids used perhaps in a deliberately limited way to support a status quo curriculum. The point is that microprocessors are already problematic for society and its youngest generation but that they will need to be accepted as such by the majority of teachers if they are taken to assist the kinds of curriculum change which Golby and others envisage.

Commonality, standards and accountability

As discussed, so far as pressures for commonality are concerned, there is the impression from the DES that the primary age range is less problematic than the secondary. The key discussion paper, *Curriculum 11–16*, makes this explicit. The HMI discussion paper, *A View of the Curriculum*, (1980a), dealt with primary education very much from the point of view of individual differences and the commonality of learning needs in its introductory section, and the curricular implications have to be drawn from this discussion:

At one level of generality, all children in primary schools need to be occupied in a programme that will enable them:
to engage with other children and with adults in a variety of working and
    social relationships;

to increase their range and understanding of English, and particularly to
   develop their ability and inclination to read and write for information
   and imaginative stimulation;
to acquire better physical control when they are writing, or exercising
   utilitarian skills and engaging in imaginative expression in art, music,
   drama or movement generally. *(p. 7)*

They comment that, stated in these general terms, the primary
curriculum seems well established and shows close conformity
among schools as a whole. There might be differences in terms of
children's individual learning needs so the emphasis is placed on
pedagogy rather than on the content on learning. There is also
considerable emphasis on skills and with using English as the main
skill. The paper is explicit about what English should include, and
likewise mathematics: 'priority should be given to acquiring
familiarity with whole numbers up to 100 by gaining skills in
relating them to one another – including the speedy recall of the
commonly used addition, multiplication, subtraction and division
facts – and by applying them to circumstances that occur in
everyday life'. (p. 9) Under their heading of 'Content and
Concepts', they outline the main activities in history, geography
and science with an emphasis on pedagogy and with the relations
between children's characteristics, teachers' knowledge and the
availability of resources being the starting point. The discussion is
in terms of the 1978 survey and there is apparent agreement on
what constitutes the primary curriculum:

Current practice is such that discussion of the primary school curriculum
does not need to concern itself so much with the total range of work as with
the extent to which parts of the curriculum are developed, especially for the
more able children. *(DES 1980a, p. 11)*

The secondary curriculum is dealt with in much more detail and
with several aspects being seen as raising problems in contrast to
their comments on the primary curriculum. It is the general
conclusions that policy formation in the direction of commonality
is revealed:

It (the paper) assumes a fairly lengthy subsequent process of consultation,
locally and nationally, to establish broad policies on the structure of the

curriculum as a whole and to develop a range of documents further defining the parts of the curriculum and their relationship to each other. These will need to take the form of statements identifying necessary skills and knowledge. There is already useful experience on which to draw of the co-operation necessary to the local formulation of curricular statements. In a number of LEA areas, working parties of teachers and LEA advisors and inspectors have produced guidelines, particularly for mathematics; some local schemes have effectively brought schools and industry and commerce together in considering curricular content and necessary skills. *(DES 1980a, p. 23)*

The DES paper, *The School Curriculum* (1981), was the last full pronouncement on the curriculum for the whole statutory age range in the series of papers beginning with *Curriculum 11–16* in 1977. It draws on the two DES surveys of primary and secondary schools, and again the secondary phase is treated in much more detail than is the primary. While the primary discussion is close to that expressed in *A View of the Curriculum*, the secondary discussion is more hard-edged in its consideration of the need for particular subjects and its concern for the fragmented appearance of the secondary curriculum. In the section entitled 'The Way Forward' it stresses the need for all schools to embark on rational appraisals of their curricula, to analyse aims and as a matter of routine to consider their work in terms of whether or not it is achieving the aims. Again, it is up to local authorities to formulate policy and be responsible for carrying it out in partnership with schools and with the DES. In the event, the atmosphere of compulsion detectable in earlier papers such as *A Framework for the Curriculum* (1980b), is toned down in favour of consultation, collaboration and partnership.

All this needs to be seen in relation to increasing pressure from central government, not for something as direct as central control which is counter to the organization of education in Britain, but for the increased accountability of local authorities, schools and teachers. Lawton (1980) suggests that 1976 was the watershed for this pressure: the tenth report of the House of Commons Expenditure Committee was concerned with the financing of education and the DES lack of control over how money was spent by local authorities.

Education should give value for money; teachers alone should not have the power over curriculum decision making which they traditionally exerted. In 1976 Prime Minister Callaghan opened the so-called Great Debate through his speech at Ruskin College when he called for reappraisals of the education service. Lawton maintains that by the end of 1976 the issues were clear: the very large sums of money being spent on education should be producing better-trained and educated young people; education should be more concerned with the needs of industry and parents should have more say in the running of schools. In 1977 the Auld Report was published on the William Tyndale School affair; it marked a discrediting of what were popularly understood as progressive methods and a swing towards more formal methods being approved of in primary schools. In the same year the Schools Council's constitution was redrafted in order to reduce teachers' power in its committees, and the DES published its Green Paper, *Education in Schools: a Consultative Document*, which suggested that while the partnership between local authorities and the DES should continue, power should be focused more from the centre. Lawton says that in 1978:

a clear conflict of interests had emerged over the control of the curriculum, essentially the secondary school curriculum. On the one hand, teachers repeatedly declared their legitimate desire for professional autonomy; on the other hand, wider demands were made for participation and accounta-bility in education, with special reference to the curriculum. *(Lawton 1980, p. 25)*

Accountability is crucial to this discussion since the issue of standards is the obverse side of the coin, regarding pressure for commonality in the curriculum; it is the means by which the curriculum can be rendered manageable by teachers and schools and can thereby be justified to the funders of educational provision. At the same time the absence of a national curriculum makes the question of standards even more acute: how will it be possible to know whether what is being taught is appropriate, or if it is being taught effectively enough for acceptable standards of learning to be achieved? One answer is simply to rely on the professional responsibility of teachers but there is a half-buried tradition of direct accountability for standards dating back to the Revised Code in the second half of the nineteenth century and only ending with the abolition of the elementary school by the 1944 Education Act.

But is accountability only linked to the achieving of certain standards? In the eyes of many teachers this is its nature, but Becher, Eraut and Knight (1981) distinguish between moral, professional and contractual accountability as being three different types which have specific implications when each is applied to teachers. Moral accountability is central to the teacher–pupil relationship while professional accountability refers to established and acceptable practices in classrooms to which new teachers are introduced to enable them to become competent practitioners. Contractual accountability concerns the obligation to render account to employers in the sense that teachers are answerable for their actions to those who are affected by them. Stressing this aspect comes close to requiring teachers to achieve particular standards of learning in the classroom if they are to fulfil their contractual obligations. This notion of accountability is dominant in the USA where by 1974 forty states had plans at various stages of operation for achieving learning objectives; all of them included legislation. Lacy and Lawton (1981) describe the behavioural performance objectives approach to public accountability as a technique derived from industry and of dubious value in its new context. President Johnson was so impressed by the running of the Department of Defense according to the manner in which the Ford Motor Company was run that he required all government departments to adopt the management objectives approach. It was an attractive means by which non-experts could control the experts. A version of this, performance contracting, had a brief popularity in the late 1960s in the USA. A contract would be drawn up between schools and a private organization in a school district in which the experts would undertake to raise the level of measurable achievement in the schools. The organization would earn its fee according to how long it took and how high the levels reached. The plan was a failure, since it was open to abuse. Like their English nineteenth-century predecessors the teachers taught the tests when they were leaked to them by dishonest employees of the organizations.

As an example of what is possible, Lacey and Lawton cite the

Michigan State accountability scheme. It has six main features: the defining of goals; the translation of these into objectives; the assessing of school needs to meet the objectives; testing what are termed 'alternative delivery systems'; developing a local evaluation capability; and using feedback from the results to guide state and local practices. Clearly, it follows the Tyler rational curriculum planning model. Since teachers' tenure in the USA is less secure than that of teachers in Britain, a strategy such as this is threatening to American teachers in a way that is hard to envisage here. But it effectively illustrates a particular view of curriculum evaluation that stresses that evaluation can be carried out only through the assessment of children's measurable achievement.

Lawton has warned that if the work of the Assessment of Performance Unit was linked to this view of accountability a similar situation could develop in Britain. Many local authorities have designed checklist schemes based on specific items or objectives to guide teachers' self-assessment, the ILEA's *Keeping the School Under Review* being a good example. It is possible to see these as potential enhancers of teachers' professionality since they tend to aim at teachers' all-round performance rather than being narrowly conceived results-getters. This impression has been reinforced by such work as the Cambridge Accountability Study, the East Sussex Accountability Project and the Evaluation of Testing in Schools Project, all of which have investigated the idea of accountability and its implications for teachers as professionals. School-based evaluation is a particularly important aspect. There is a clear linkage between a professionally orientated idea of accountability and the enhancement of teachers' professional status through their being responsible for evaluation in their own schools, both because of the particular skills needed, and because of the quality of the responsibility being invested in teachers. This is in sharp contrast to the image of the technician-teacher as a worker on an educational production line. Sockett (1980) and others have argued for the professional model of accountability in which the emphasis is on the development of the understanding of the principles underlying effective practice rather than simply on getting results. He sees the distinction as follows:

(a)   accountability would be *for* adherence to principles of practice rather than *for* results embodied in pupil performances.

(b)   accountability would be rendered *to* diverse constituencies rather than *to* the agglomerate constituency of the public alone.

(c)   the teacher would have to be regarded as an autonomous professional, not as a social technician, within the bureaucratic framework of a school and the education system.

(d)   the evaluation through measurement of pupil performances (the 'how' of accountability) would be replaced by the conception of evaluation as providing information to constituents allied to a system of proper redress through a professional body.   *(Sockett 1980, p. 19)*

In short, teachers would be accountable in the same way as other professionals. Of course this is only procedural in the absence of self-government through a professional organization such as a Teachers' Council, though the conception of accountability adopted by local authorities resembles this model. Sockett suggests that in order for this conception to be developed further, teachers would need self-government with all that this entails in terms of a defined code of conduct in all areas of professional activity from direct classroom responsibilities to participation in school government. Sockett also asserts that teachers as professionals must be concerned with the ways in which teachers are promoted into administrative positions and with the development of close relationships with researchers and theorists concerned with evaluation techniques and methods.

Teachers, then, should welcome accountability since it acknowledges their importance and their professional status. With the gradual achievement of an all-graduate profession another aspect of developed professionality seems to be secure. However it seems to be tacit policy for central government to resist the idea of a teachers' governing body since, without it, teachers can be treated like any other group of local authority employees.

Summary

Though it might be the case that general arguments about the content of the primary curriculum have been settled, there are a number of issues that make their claims on teachers. These include the integration of children with special needs into ordinary schools, developing curricula which is multicultural rather than ethnocentric, equal opportunities between boys and girls to achieve in all aspects of the curriculum and the impact of new technology on primary schools. A more pervasive issue is that of curriculum commonality and the consequent debates about educational standards and teachers' for accountability for maintaining these.

The formal position of children with special needs is clear following the publication of the Warnock Report in 1978 and the Education Act of 1981. A range of necessary provisions is recognized including integrating children as far as possible into the mainstream of education. Several of the problems for teachers and for pupils have been revealed by recent research. The curricular implications rest on how far a normal curriculum can be implemented and what kinds of adjustments to the mainstream will be needed for different children. A major problem is the labelling of children with special needs. This social pathology approach has several implications: teachers' expectations will vary and, with these, the learning levels of pupils, with the danger of a 'therapeutic' and therefore inferior conception of education being implemented.

The position is similar with children from ethnic minorities and for girls. The social pathology view through labelling is likely to convey to teachers what can be expected of certain children because of their covert handicaps they inherit through being members of an ethnic minority or being girls. The early assimilationist policy towards children from other cultures has given way to an integrationalist stance. Both can be seen as discriminatory, leading to educational experiences that are designed to compensate children for their cultural 'handicaps'. Cultural diversity at least attempts to recognize difference but can be prone to tokenism and naiveness on the part of teachers. Terms such as 'immigrant' and 'race' are often used inaccurately and with strong cultural charges. Negative self-image is often held up as being the main barrier to learning on the part of Afro-Caribbean children, but this has been contested.

Again with girls, there has been a confusion between the biological and the cultural unwittingly aided by early research into child development and which justifies as being 'natural' the differential achievement in aspects of the curriculum between boys and girls. The actual curriculum is often strongly reinforced by the hidden curriculum by which the conduct of boys and girls is distinguished. What is crucial about all of these issues is the attitudes of teachers: implicit racism and sexism need to be recognized for what they are and eradicated, as a first move towards developing curricula which respect equal opportunity in all its manifestations.

So far as what is termed the new technology is concerned, teachers need to recognize children's familiarity with it outside classrooms and to treat it as being problematic to them in terms of the skills they need to operate with it.

The range of papers produced by the DES and HMI since 1977 seem to regard the primary curriculum as being less Issue-fraught than the secondary. The emphasis in the primary curriculum discussions is placed on pedagogy rather than curriculum content, with the primary survey providing the main reference points. The satisfaction of individual differences and common learning needs is at the core of the discussion. Since the issue of standards is the obverse side of the coin in the commonality debate, accountability is central; it has different conceptual meanings and different implications for teachers. At its most instrumental, the concern is for maintaining standards by achieving prespecified objectives, as in the American model, while professional accountability is geared to the introduction of new teachers to established and acceptable practices in classrooms in order that they become competent practitioners. In Britain there appears to be a basic respect on the part of local authorities for teachers' professionality. However, this is only partly acknowledged by those authorities which are adopting performance objectives accountability strategies. Teachers' professional standing will be enhanced in this respect only in those situations where they are made fully responsible for carrying out school self-assessment programmes.

Further Reading

Deem, R. (1978), *Women and Schooling.* London: Routledge and Kegan Paul
  Overview of sexism in schooling.

Hegarty, S., Pocklington, K. and Lucas, D. (1981), *Educating Pupils with Special Needs in the Ordinary School*, Slough: NFER/Nelson

James, A. and Jeffcoate, R. (eds.) (1981), *The School in the Multicultural Society*, London: Harper and Row
Curriculum-orientated papers on aspects of planning and provision.

Lacey, C. and Lawton, D. (eds.) (1981), *Issues in Evaluation and Accountability*, London: Methuen
Examines the links between evaluation and forms of accountability.

7. Curriculum commonality: the key issues

The 'administrators' and the 'educators'

There have been many references so far to the overarching issue of curriculum commonality, and to the contrasting perspectives of what have been termed the 'administrators', which broadly represents the DES view, and the 'educators' which refers to the academic theorists concerned with this issue. It has been pointed out that pressures for commonality have focused on the secondary school as being most in need of reform. While the 'administrators' are concerned broadly with economic investment and efficiency arguments, the 'educators' have developed epistemological and social justice arguments supporting their proposals. Of course, this distinction over-simplifies the position, and in practice there are overlaps, since the 'educators' are not blind to the more enlightened social utility views on educational provision and the 'administrators' are well aware of and generally align themselves with social justice viewpoints.

Even a superficial reading of both groups' arguments reveals a deep discontent with the structure and content of the secondary curriculum on a number of grounds. It is haphazard between schools regarding curriculum coverage and balance, it is too dominated by examination systems, it encourages over-specialization too early, it is over-traditional in emphasizing academic subjects, and it is out of date in that it does not address the present and likely future needs of many young people in the 14 to 19 years age range. All this adds up to a poor preparation immediately beyond school both for employment and its alternatives, and for further education, either vocational or non-vocational, in colleges, polytechnics and universities. There is the obvious fact of secondary schooling being an important part of the interface between school and adult life, and therefore a more acute concern is felt by educationalists for its procedures and practices.

It is significant, for instance, that one major theorist, Lawton, does not discuss the primary curriculum in either of the books in which develops his views on commonality. His whole concern is for the secondary school years and the inadequacies, as he sees them, of the secondary school curriculum. White (1973) in his more extreme arguments for a compulsory curriculum is also concerned for similar reasons with the secondary curriculum. Hirst, too, from his first essay to his later writings (1965; 1970; 1974) is concerned with developing a basis for a common curriculum through his theory of the forms of knowledge and this is tacitly at least for the secondary school.

The only educator to develop a detailed common curriculum proposal for primary education is Dearden (1968). It is true that the Schools Council Middle Years of Schooling Project also produced a ground plan for the 8 to 13 years age range, in junior and middle schools and the lower classes of secondaries. None of the papers produced by the DES and HMI from 1977 to 1981 considers a possible common primary school curriculum in anything like the detail bestowed on secondary education, though by inference and extrapolation from the primary survey in 1978, the ground work for such a proposal can be seen. Similar things could be said about the Plowden Committee in its discussion of the subjects it identifies as representing the primary curriculum. Also the ORACLE findings have uncovered a form of tacitly agreed curriculum which might be termed common and which is practised independently of each other by teachers in their own classrooms. The Schools Council in its working paper 70, *The Practical Curriculum* (1981), formulated a structure for curriculum appraisal by teachers which spanned the statutory age range of schooling and in doing so gave due emphasis to the range and progression of skills and conceptual understanding which characterizes modern primary education. It is notable that the analysis and proposals were not stated in terms of subjects and disciplines but took the processes operating in primary classrooms as being the organizational underpinning. This is not of course a developed, grand design-type proposal, but the subsequent Working Paper 75, *Primary Practice* (1983), is a considerable elaboration of the initial position.

This then seems to be the position. The DES is satisfied with the general curriculum coverage it has surveyed but wants it extended to all schools and classrooms and for teachers to become more competent in teaching subjects such as science. Teachers teach a form of common curriculum which in its emphasis represents the DES idea of an 'irreducible core' made up of language and mathematics, which they acquired during their training and which was confirmed as their stock-in-trade in the early years of their teaching. A very few educationalists have addressed themselves to the possibilities of a common primary curriculum, or a curriculum which includes the primary years.

While commonality has been discussed earlier in terms of what it implies for teachers' accountability, there are good reasons for considering the notion as an attempt by individuals and groups representing different interests, viewpoints and perhaps value positions to define the primary curriculum. All such attempts are by nature prescriptive and stand as recommendations for improvement of the status quo. In taking this standpoint, they either implicitly or explicitly stress the role of teachers as curriculum decision-makers in the whole school as well as the classroom context. Proposals need to be cashed in terms of whole school schemes and guidelines which require collaborative effort on the part of staff. This is very much the DES viewpoint, seen in its clearest form in the review of Circular 14/77, published in 1979. All of these attempts, then, postulate an extension of teachers' classroom responsibilities which has the potential effect of enhancing their professionality. In turn, this raises questions about the nature and direction of school-based curriculum development and school-focused in-service teacher education which are in the process of being resolved as the schools respond to the requirement that they produce their own curriculum schemes and guidelines. This important development was brought about by Circular 14/77 which required that local authorities produce curricular guidelines for use in their schools. A major implication of this for schools is that they are now in a position of having to justify their curricular decision-making to an increasingly informed and knowledgeable public. The Taylor Committee in 1977 was instrumental in broadening the composition of school governing bodies to include parents and in allowing entry to classrooms to governors. Schools are also required to develop information systems and to produce annual booklets for parents which explain the curriculum and the school rules.

In this highly complex situation the DES would seem to have limited room for manoeuvre in that it must formulate and guide policy by oblique means in order to respect the autonomy of local authorities, schools and teachers. Hence the discussion and policy-forming documents, reports on sectors of provision and White Papers and consultatives documents such as the recent one on teacher quality. However, this room can be extended where the DES is able to demonstrate through its own research investigations that there are shortcomings in the education system which justify less oblique initiatives.

Curriculum commonality: Circular 14/77

It can be seen from the arguments in the earlier chapters that most of the pressures for change in primary education stem from increasing concern for curriculum content and management. This curriculum orientation is in contrast with the traditional child-centred concern for teaching methods and classroom organization as noted in Chapter 3. It can be discerned at the level of the DES by the range of discussion and policy documents published after *Curriculum 11-16* in 1977. At the level of the local education authorities there is a concern to devise schemes for all primary curriculum areas, while at the school and teachers' level, there is an increasing awareness of the need to plan curriculum units and to be responsible for evaluating as well as implementing them. The trend at the school level is marked by the recognition of the need for curriculum leadership: of assigning scale posts for responsibility for organizing an aspect of the curriculum. The general ineffectiveness of such leaders to influence their colleagues was noted in the primary survey, though the five years following its publication have seen a considerable tightening up of procedures for defining and implementing curricula in schools. This should have the effect of strengthening the authority of scale post-holders as consultants and as leaders of change in their schools.

Overarching this marked curriculum orientation has been an increasing concern on the part of the DES to define at least a protected core, so to speak, of essential skills to be inculcated through the curriculum. Some of the thinking behind the more outspoken papers has been discussed here, especially in Chapter 6. They have their origins in the review of DES Circular 14/77, *Local Authority Arrangements for the School Curriculum* (1979). It represesents the intention to play a more direct part in decision-making initially through finding out by a survey how well the local authorities were carrying out the responsibilities invested in them by the 1944 Education Act, and then using this information to bring pressure to bear on them to produce curriculum guidelines for schools which would meet the Department's approval. Underlying this drive towards commonality of content as well as range there is a regard for standards:

The Education Acts lay the responsibility of providing efficient and sufficient primary and secondary education to meet the needs of their areas firmly on local education authorities. As with central government, this implies a concern by authorities with the content and quality of education as well as with the facilities which they provide. To fulfill their responsibilities effectively within any nationally agreed framework authorities must exercise leadership and interpret national policies and objectives in the light of local needs and circumstances. *(p. 3)*

If each local authority is to interpret what the DES requires by developing guidelines which its schools are to implement, then the DES is in the position where it can stop well short of making a bid for central control of the school curriculum. In not doing this, the delicate coalition of interests represented by the distribution of power between the Department and the local education authorities remains intact. No wholesale change will take place, but the DES will be in the position of controlling the curriculum through its success in getting LEAs to operate according to curriculum guidelines which it has laid down. And these are no more than outlines; and although some of the survey questions in 14/77 seem to make suggestions as to what subjects should be represented in the secondary curriculum, there is probably no need for the DES to go further than this, since it has achieved curriculum control simply by ensuring that curriculum policy-making, planning and resourcing by local authorities is made public and explicit in a manner which has not been seen since the centrally administered Board of Education Codes ceased in 1926. The DES is quite clear about its intentions:

> The Secretaries of State do not seek to determine in detail what the schools should teach or how it should be taught; but they have an inescapable duty to satisfy themselves that the work of the schools matches national needs. *(Circular 14/77 Review, p. 2)*

It is also clear from the Review that while local authorities are required to 'formulate curriculum policies and objectives', schools will use them to guide their own policy-making rather than the local authorities imposing direct control through them on school curricula.

This advice is surprising in its moderation considering how little authorities know, it was revealed in the survey, about the curriculum operating in their schools. One-fifth reported that they made an annual collection of curriculum and organizational information from their secondary schools. A quarter gained some information through analysing external examination entries, while a further fifth relied on head teachers' annual reports to their governing bodies as a source of information. But only one-tenth of the authorities regularly collected detailed curriculum information from some of their primary schools. Also, the notion of policy-making itself seemed to apply to decision-making at any level within the area for many local authorities, and few at the time were producing detailed curriculum statements. Significantly, one-sixth of authorities said that this could lead to undue restrictions on teachers in the exercise of their professional judgement.

The survey, then, provided the DES with information about local authority practices which it found disquietening. While the authorities were carrying out their legal responsibilities, they tended to take the same general, unanalysed viewpoint on the school curriculum as that expressed in the 1944 Act. The DES response was to take a hard line:

They [the Secretaries of State] believe they should seek to give a lead in the process of reaching a rational consensus on a desirable framework for the curriculum and consider the development of such a framework a priority for the education service . . . . Such a framework will need to relate to the broad shape of the whole curriculum for the various stages of school education, and be capable of flexibility in accordance with changing perceptions over time of individual and social needs. It would give central government a firmer basis for the development of rational policies and the deployment of resources; and provide a check-list for authorities and schools in formulating and reviewing their curricular aims and policies in the light of local needs and circumstances, and for teachers in exercising their professional skills and extending the interests of their pupils. (*Circular 14/77 Review, pp. 6-7*)

As an initial step, the discussion paper *A View of the Curriculum* was published in 1980, but so far none of the more radical decisions, which would in effect locate curriculum decision-making with the DES instead of the local authorities, have been taken.

By contrast, the 'educators' position is relatively issue-free. It is interesting that the two most comprehensive and widely known both derive from the Plowden Report. Dearden's proposals stem from his criticisms of its child-centred ideology which has led him to take a curriculum orientated view in attempting to realize the dominant aim of promoting individual autonomy which he argues is implicit in the report's reasoning. The Middle Years of Schooling scheme arises from an acceptance of the report's rationale.

Curriculum commonality: the 'educators'

Dearden begins his argument with a critique of the Plowden Report's account of the aims of primary education, which he largely

dismisses in favour of the aims which he argues are implicit in the
committee's notion of primary education and the child as learner.
He then considers the report's discussion of the curriculum which
he criticizes for its subjects basis: there are problems to do with the
claimed arbitrary nature of subjects, as discussed in Chapter 1, and
these raise difficulties as to the criteria for selecting subjects:

Would it be simplicity, logical priority, motivational appeal, social utility,
examinability? And if that were settled, would the result not be a
compartmentalisation which was arbitrary from every point of view except
that of the convenience of university teaching and research? *(Dearden
1968, p. 3)*

He moves on to consider what educational content would possibly
satisfy the aims of personal autonomy based on reason which he
maintains are implicit in Plowden. He suggests that a Hirstian
forms of knowledge approach is preferable to an attempt to
formulate a curriculum from subjects. Five forms of understanding
are necessary: mathematical, scientific, historical, aesthetic, and
ethical. For him, the structure of a form of knowledge has two
elements: they are systems of interconnected concepts and organizing
principles and for each of them there are validation procedures by
which the truth, rightness and adequacy of their ideas can be
determined. He maintains that 'Knowledge in this sense is not a
seamless robe, but rather a coat of many colours. Far from being
'divorced from life', it slowly transforms our very notions of
ourselves, of 'life' and of 'the world'.' *(Dearden 1968, p. 63)*
   Children's understanding would come from guided discovery
and not rote learning through their being able to use the forms as a
structure in which to develop and elaborate their thinking. First-
hand experience is crucial to this kind of understanding. He then
considers the curricular implications of his five forms of understanding in much the same way that Hirst set about developing his
seven forms of knowledge. In Dearden's analysis the forms become
mathematics, science, history, the arts, ethics and religion, and in
defending these as a basis for primary education he claims that:

the forms of understanding above mentioned are basic ways in which
human experience has, as a matter of fact, been extended and elaborated in

the course of history. Such understanding is therefore presupposed by rational choice and hence is of great relevance to formal education, of which it is in special need for its transmission. *(p. 79)*

From his analysis Dearden argues that the primary school curriculum firstly should be organized to take account of the first four forms of understanding. Second, what he calls 'basic skills' should be identified: he sees these as being the mechanics of reading and writing, verbal skills in English and some procedures in arithmetic which have social utility and on which other parts of the curriculum depend. He stresses that these would need to be constantly reviewed in the light of their use to children. He also includes those skills which are needed to produce work which is publically legible and intelligible and argues that map reading is important enough in our society for it to be a basic skill. Third, physical education should be added in the form of the normal range of activities such as games, gymnastics, swimming and health education. He considers that his fifth form of understanding, ethics is learned through the other forms and is also implicit in the life of the school through its hidden curriculum. He then briefly suggests how this discipline-based curriculum might be put into operation. Religious education in its present form would be replaced by what he calls 'incidental teaching *about* religion' through literature, history and social studies. English would also disappear as a single subject to be replaced by basic language skills and aspects of aesthetic education which call for language. He is critical of comprehension as a skill since it is isolated and does not transfer as do the skills that he is proposing and he has similar doubts about grammar. What he calls 'a loose federation of natural and human sciences' would be recognized as geography. Craft in terms of boys' handwork and girls' needlework which still lingers on, especially in top classes in junior schools, would be replaced by 'domestic skills' such as gardening, carpentry, cooking and needlework for all children. Craft work would figure in mathematics activities and in art and history.

So far as organization is concerned, he makes a plea for the sort of informal semi-specialization that can be developed through a team or a co-operative teaching approach and through appointing staff to curriculum leadership posts in school on the basis of their acknowledged expertise in different parts of the curriculum. General schemes would need to be compiled for the whole curriculum which would be organized through blocks of time. This would avoid the rigid timetabling of the subjects-based curriculum and the too-open endedness of the integrated day, though curriculum integration is possible in Dearden's ground plan:

One form of understanding often enters into another, but in a properly subsidiary role. In making a historical drawing, say of a galleon, aesthetic considerations are relevant, but ought to be subordinated to an appropriate degree of historical accuracy, or else history becomes a pretty little phantasy. Again, mathematics enters into most things, and there is no suggestion that it should not. Aesthetic considerations come into the basic skills, as when italic handwriting is taught, and so on. *(pp. 91-2)*

Some of what Dearden suggests is inevitably dated from its inception in 1968. There is no mention, for example, of special needs or a concern for multicultural or gender issues. But a good deal of what he says could be accepted as good practice, or even as being innovatory, in many junior schools. In fact it reads very much like a curriculum for the junior school, for children aged 7 to 11 years, rather than encompassing the infant and junior age range. He goes on to consider play as an educational process and is inclined to dismiss its claims as being not proven on empirical and epistemological grounds. But, he goes a good deal further than most theorists in trying to cash his views in practical terms. It could also be conceded that he begs some fundamental questions about the nature of primary education in proposing a strongly curriculum orientated account. His earlier analysis of the Plowden proposals for child-centred education amounts to a strong critique but as well as attacking this view of primary education, he is equally critical of over-controlled and teacher directed formal views with their over-emphasis on subjects and assessable skills. Some of his elaborated forms of understanding begin to look like subjects in the same way the Hirst's forms of knowledge take on a subjects appearance when used as a basis for curriculum planning. Again, Dearden has developed an all-inclusive curriculum but can it be claimed that his five forms contain the sum total of human understanding into which primary children will be initiated, or do these merely reduce human understanding to five manageable portions? The charge of reductionism has been levelled at Hirst also, as it can be at any disciplines-based scheme.

Another attempt to formulate a common curriculum is that of the Schools Council Middle Years of Schooling Project. It is not strictly speaking concerned with the primary age range but with the 8 to 13 years age range partly represented in junior schools. The general arguments set out in Working Paper 42, *Education in the Middle Years* (1972), and developed in the final report of the project, Working Paper 55, *The Curriculum in the Middle Years* (1975). The project team compared the heavily subject-orientated accounts of curriculum in the 1905 Handbook of Suggestions to Teachers, the Ministry of Education guide to primary education published in 1959, and the ultimately subjects-based scheme in Plowden. The lists are remarkably similar and indicate the fixed nature of the primary curriculum both in official eyes and in the eyes of teachers. Each defines what was seen at the time as a model of primary education, partly through reflecting current practice and partly through trying to refine this. The Middle Years team favoured a holistic approach to curriculum planning and acknowledged the role of curriculum experts in developing this. It is also by implication against the idea of subjects:

Educationalists have recognised for a very long time that careful planning of the curriculum involves a consideration of what to leave out as well as what to include, but have, until recently, limited this consideration chiefly to facts and skills. It is *this* kind of curriculum that is reasonably easy to produce. It involves no more than making a balanced selection of items from the different areas of the curriculum and setting them out in fairly precise terms; it is also easy to categorise them. *(Working Paper 42, p. 54)*

If this paper is the ground-clearing operation, its companion paper sets out the conclusions and how they were arrived at:

The point of view taken in this chapter is firstly that any curriculum should be the result of conscious planning as well as intuition, and secondly, that planning is of particular importance in middle years education since these

years are so important in the development of the child as a thinking
person. *(Working Paper 55, p. 11)*

The team is at pains not to alienate child-centred teachers who
might consider that planning in any sense of the term is inimical to
child-centredness. After a discussion of aims where it confirms the
broadly child-centred aims in a social context which permeates
Plowden, it considers the range of learning theories that might
inform the planning of children's learning experiences. An eclectic
view is taken since it would be unrealistic to claim that any one
learning theory could encompass all children's learning activities.

The team then moves on to content in terms of the kinds of
conceptual structures from which a curriculum for the middle
years might be generated. This begins from what appears to be a
disciplines approach. Four content areas are suggested: basic
learning skills, empirical studies, aesthetics, and morality. Subjects
are then allocated to these according to where each can make the
strongest contribution and with the acknowledgement that many
subjects can contribute to several areas. For example, in empirical
studies, the contributing subjects are history, geography, science,
social studies and nature study, realized through projects and
environmental studies schemes. The team is more concerned with
the mode of learning in the content area than with the contributing
subjects. For younger children the content could be integrated in an
umbrella subject like environmental studies, but for children aged
12 and 13 years, the team envisages a distinction being drawn
between science as a separate subject and the group of subjects
loosely making up social studies.

Aesthetics includes art, craft, drama, literature, movement and
physical education, while morality is not seen as a separate subject
but is included in health education, moral education, religious
education and parts of history, geography and literature. Alongside
these the hidden curriculum of the school will be influential.
Although the team is concerned to link its thinking with that of
Hirst and Phenix, the overall impression is one of separate,
traditional subjects being marshalled under rough and ready
headings rather than the tightly argued conceptual schemes of
these two theorists. As a curriculum proposal it is not as radical as

Dearden's, being little more than a restatement of the status quo. What characterizes it is its explicit curriculum planning basis. The team stresses the rational process of curriculum planning and the part that teachers must play in implementing the scheme. Such planning is a sophisticated and unfamiliar task for teachers; team members reported that while many junior school heads and teachers were prepared to discuss in detail the reasons why they had adopted vertical grouping or integrated days, they were less prepared to discuss the content and planning of the curriculum. Clearly, what was important here was the teachers' traditional right to decide the curriculum for their classes. Since curriculum planning can be an isolating activity, the team, apropos of Miles, suggested a group approach be adopted for planning. However, while planning might be a group activity, implementation was seen as being an individual business.

Much of what the team says about planning, implementation and the nature of innovation is commonsensical, being based on members' school experience and being well supported in the research literature. The scheme itself is interesting only because of the scarcity of such schemes: there is little in it which would offend any but the most conservative teachers; what is new is the rational and organised approach to curriculum planning.

Curriculum commonality: further issues

There are a number of questions which have yet to be settled which are basic to commonality. The matter of who decides has been considered in some detail here, but it raises the further issue of how far would it be possible for schools in markedly different localities to be able to respond to what they see as different educational needs; how far does commonality imply uniformity? There is the related question, perhaps more powerful in its implications, of standards of attainment. If commonality is open to different interpretations to meet different needs, how could it be assured that children throughout the country were reaching adequate standards of understanding and attainment? This of course presupposes that adequate standards in all areas of the curriculum for the different age groups could be agreed upon by the DES, local authorities and teachers. Lawton has considered this issue in connection with his arguments for a common culture curriculum for the secondary school; it is so fraught with subjectivity and problems of justification, even when considered only in terms of the basic skills, that the problem of establishing agreed standards appears to be insurmountable. Again, would standards, if they could be agreed upon, act as guidelines for teachers or would they be binding in some way, in the interests of accountability?

It is clear that the DES is not seeking a grand design-type solution to curriculum commonality for a number of reasons advanced here earlier. What is crucial to future developments in schools is the balance to be decided between curriculum planning and the requirements of accountability. Since direct intervention is unlikely, in spite of the existence of the Assessment of Performance Unit, this balance will be decided by the individual local authorities, guided by the DES.

A further, and over-arching question concerns the implementation of equal rights policies, broadly encouraged by the DES and beginning to find expression through local authority policy-making. Where teachers might feel relatively neutral about curriculum content and its sequencing and resourcing, issues to do with class, race, gender and special needs engage with teachers' personal beliefs which, while being private, inevitably have a formative and directing influence over their professional practice. On the face of it, teachers might claim the right as citizens to hold personal social and moral views which do not agree with the social and moral stance held by their employers, the local authorities. An example might be a politically moderate teacher or head-teacher who believes in a gradualist policy of implementation being faced with implementing policies of a radical, social engineering nature. The range of possible standpoints on the development of a multicultural curriculum, for instance, is considerable. Who is to define what is right and with what moral authority?

There is also the question of the status of school-based curriculum development and in-service teacher education in a system where local authority guidelines are authoritative if they are not binding.

The spirit of the DES recommendations is broadly in favour of teacher autonomy exercised within the parameters established by the requirement that local authorities guide schools in directions indicated by the DES. This style of operating is essentially liberal and consultative as it is presently conducted; it could become authoritarian and interventionist if a narrowly conceived notion of accountability was applied, or where the idea of a protected core of basic skills in language and mathematics was imposed on teachers. There is the question, too, of the role of HMIs in a school and local authority-centred curriculum development situation. Much still depends on how individual local authorities interpret and implement their curricular responsibilities but on the face of it, schools and teachers are being encouraged to innovate in a way which was lacking in the 1960s and 1970s when the curriculum development scene was dominated by the large-scale Schools Council projects. The voluntary principle which operated then meant that innovation was often a piecemeal activity carried out by solitary teachers in their own classrooms. The element of compulsion which now applies means that a school staff working together need to inquire into how far the whole curriculum is meeting the needs of their children and what changes to make if it is ineffective in any way. There is still the problem, however, in this new spirit of planning, that accountability schemes which operate with performance objectives will be in considerable tension with school-based curriculum development. Since many local authorities perceive accountability in terms of objectives which teachers will achieve, however they are presented, clashes between curriculum development activities and the demands of accountability appear to be inevitable.

It is still possible, nevertheless, to see the DES initiative as pointing directly at teacher's professionality and at the need for teachers to accept the responsibility to innovate at a time when the exercise of their judgement is being subjected to many competing demands. If the curriculum is the medium through which teachers engage children in learning, it cannot be artificially reduced to that learning which can readily be measured in the interests of accountability; nor can it be entirely decided by teachers operating independently in their own classrooms.

Summary

The main emphasis regarding curriculum commonality has been placed on the secondary school because of the continuing criticisms of secondary education on the part of the 'administrators' and the 'educators'. There is the assumption that the primary curriculum is satisfactory but needs developing and consolidating. Recent surveys and research have revealed what is in effect a common primary curriculum, emphasizing basic skills in language and mathematics and taught by teachers independently of each other.

While commonality has been discussed earlier in connection with teacher accountability, it is also important in itself because of the attempts by various groups and individuals to define the primary school curriculum. The position of teachers here is important since such attempts tend to stress their roles as curriculum decision-makers working with their colleagues in formulating whole school policies.

The DES appears on the face of it to have little room for manoeuvre in this situation, since it is committed to the distribution of power between it and the local authorities, which in effect recognizes their autonomy and therefore their decision-making rights. But the survey reported in the 14/77 Review revealed that the local authorities are not closely in touch with their schools regarding the curriculum taught in them; the Review makes it clear that the DES intends to take a lead in establishing curriculum guidelines from which local authorities will develop schemes to cover all aspects of the curriculum taught in schools. Although more interventionalist moves were suggested in the Review, so far, none of these have been implemented. Indeed, the DES, if it is successful in controlling the curriculum through requiring local authorities to formalize it by publishing guidelines and schemes, need do no more than this, since commonality in general terms will have been achieved through its actions.

By contrast, the 'educators' are in a position which is relatively free from issues, political or otherwise. Dearden's disciplines approach represented, in 1968, a major appraisal many of whose propositions still hold; it was an early expression of the trend for primary education to become more curriculum orientated. The

Schools Council Middle Years of Schooling Project also developed a curriculum plan for an age group, but while it was forward looking in its recognition of the need to plan, the content organization is not far removed from a conventional subjects-based scheme.

There are a number of issues to do with commonality which have yet to be settled. The question of diversity within a common curriculum framework has implications for the kinds of standards of attainment which might be expected from different schools. This presupposes that the difficult problem of establishing and getting agreement on standards could be solved. Also there are issues, particularly to do with equal opportunities policies which overarch the curriculum and which engage the personal and private views of teachers in a way which is unlike questions to do with curriculum content and its organization.

Arguably the most important issue lies in the claim that the element of compulsion in the DES policy could have the effect of broadening the primary curriculum beyond the traditional emphasis on language and mathematics because of the requirement that school staffs appraise the whole curriculum operating in a school.

Further reading

Dearden, R. (1968), *The Philosophy of Primary Education*, London: Routledge and Kegan Paul
Lawton, D. (1980), *The Politics of the School Curriculum*, London: Routledge and Kegan Paul
    Chapter 3 is a useful survey of DES initiatives on the common curriculum since 1976.
Schools Council Working Paper 70 (1981), *The Practical Curriculum*, London: Evans/Methuen.
    The Schools Council's contribution to the current debate.

Bibliography

Alexander, R. The B.Ed and the primary teacher's curriculum knowledge. Conference paper: CNAA Undergraduate Initial Training Board. *Initial B.Ed Courses for the Early and Middle Years*, West Midlands College, March 1981

Ashton, P., Kneen, P., Davies, F. and Holley, B. (1975), *The Aims of Primary Education: A Study of Teachers' Opinions*, London: MacMillan Educational

Banks, O. (1971), *The Sociology of Education*, London: Batsford

Becher, A., Eraut, M. and Knight, J. (1981), *Policies for Educational Accountability*, London: Heinemann

Bennett, N. (1976), *Teaching Styles and Pupil Progress*, London: Open Books

Bernstein, B. 'A critique of "compensatory education",' in D. Rubenstein and C. Stoneman (eds.) (1970), *Education for Democracy*, Harmondsworth: Penguin

Blyth, W. (1965), *English Primary Education* (2 vols.), London: Routledge and Kegan Paul

Boyd, J. (1977), *Community Education and Urban Schools*, London: Longman

Boydell, D. (1978), *The Primary Teacher in Action*, London: Open Books

Brennan, W. (1982), *Changing Special Education*, Bletchley: Open University Press

Brook, J., 'Teacher-based research and the classroom teacher', in C. Hannam, P. Smyth, and M. Stephenson (eds.) (1976), *The First Year of Teaching*, Harmondsworth: Penguin

Bruner, J. (1968), *Toward a Theory of Instruction*, New York: Norton

Central Advisory Council for Education (1967). (Plowden, B. Chairman), *Children and their Primary Schools* (vols. 1 and 2), London: HMSO

Committee of Enquiry into the Education of Handicapped Children and Young People (1978), (Warnock, M., Chairman), *Special Educational Needs*, London: HMSO

Curtis, S. and Boultwood, M. (1965), *A Short History of Educational Ideas*, London: University Tutorial Press

Dearden, R. 'Instruction and learning by discovery', in R. Peters (ed.) (1967), *The Concept of Education*, London: Routledge and Kegan Paul

Dearden R. (1968), *The Philosophy of Primary Education*, London: Routledge and Kegan Paul

Dearden, R. (1976), *Problems in Primary Education*, London: Routledge and Kegan Paul

Dearden, R. 'The Primary Survey: an assessment', in C. Richards, (ed.) (1980), *Primary Education: Issues for the Eighties*, London: Adam and Charles Black

Deem, R. (1978), *Women and Schooling*, London: Routledge and Kegan Paul

Department of Education and Science (1977), *Curriculum 11–16*, London: HMSO

Department of Education and Science (1979), *Local Authority Arrangements for the School Curriculum, Report on the Circular 14/77 Review;* London: HMSO

Department of Education and Science (1978), *Primary Education in England: A Survey by HM Inspectors of Schools*, London: HMSO

Department of Education and Science (1980a), *A View of the Curriculum*, HMI Series, Matters for Discussion no. 111, London: HMSO

Department of Education and Science (19806), *A Framework for the Curriculum*, London: HMSO

Department of Education and Science (1981), *The School Curriculum*, London: HMSO

Department of Education and Science (1982), *Education 5–9: an Illustrative Survey of 80 First Schools in England*, London: HMSO

Dewey, J., 'The child and the curriculum', in M. Golby, J. Greenwald and R. West (eds.) (1975), *Curriculum Design*, London: Croom Helm

Dodridge, J., 'Using micro-computers across the curriculum in a primary school', in R. Garland (ed.) (1982), *Microcomputers and Children in the Primary School*, Lewes: Falmer Press

Douglas, J. (1964), *The Home and the School*, London: MacGibbon and Kee

Eggleston, J. Introduction, in J. Eggleston (ed.) (1980), *School-based Curriculum Development in Britain*, London: Routledge and Kegan Paul

Eisner, E., 'Instructional and expressive educational objectives: their formulation and use in the curriculum', in W. Popham, E. Eisner, H. Sullivan, and L. Tyler (1969), *Instructional Objectives*, American Educational Research Association Monograph Series on Curriculum Evaluation, no. 3, Chicago: Rand MacNally

Elliot, J., 'The self-assessment of teachers' performance', in Bulletin No. 2, January 1978. Classroom Action Research Network, Cambridge: Institute of Education

Elliott, J. and Adelmann, C., 'Innovation at the classroom level: a case study of the Ford Teaching Project', in Unit 28 (1976), *Innovation, the School and the Teacher I*, E203, Milton Keynes: Open University Press

Ennever, L. *et al.* (1972), *With Objectives in Mind*, London: Macdonald Educational

Forward, R. 'A time for change', in J. Walton and J. Welton (eds.) (1976), *Rational Curriculum Planning: Four Case Studies*, London: Ward Lock Educational

Galton, M. and Simon, B. (eds.) (1980), *Progress and Performance in the Primary Classroom*, London: Routledge and Kegan Paul

Galton, M., Simon, B. and Croll, P. (1980), *Inside the Primary Classroom*, London: Routledge and Kegan Paul

Golby, M., Microcomputer and the primary curriculum', in R.

Garland (ed.) (1982), *Microcomputers and Children in the Primary School,* Lewes: Falmer Press

Goodacre, E. (1967), *Reading in Infants Classes,* Slough: NFER

Hargreaves, D., 'A phenomenological approach to classroom decision-making', in J. Eggleston (ed.) (1979), *Teacher Decision-Making in the Classroom,* London: Routledge and Kegan Paul

Harlen, W. and Elliot, J., 'A check-list for planning or reviewing an evaluation', in R. McCormick (ed.) (1982), *Calling Education to Account,* London: Heinemann

Havelock, R. (1971), *Planning by Innovation through the Dissemination and Utilization of Knowledge,* Ann Arbor: Centre for Research and Utilization of Knowledge

Hegarty, S., Pockington, K. and Lucas D. (1981), *Educating Pupils with Special Needs in the Ordinary School,* Slough: NFER/Nelson

Hirst, P., 'Liberal education and the nature of knowledge', in R. Archambault, (ed.) (1965), *Philosophical Analysis and Education,* London: Routledge and Kegan Paul

Hirst, P. (1974), *Knowledge and the Curriculum,* London: Routledge and Kegan Paul

Hirst P. and Peters, R. (1970), *The Logic of Education,* London: Routledge and Kegan Paul

Holloway, M. in R. Garland (ed.) (1982), *Microcomputers and Children in Primary Schools,* Lewes: Falmer Press

Hoyle, E. (1969), 'How does the curriculum change?' in R. Hooper (ed.) (1971), *The Curriculum: Context, Design and Development,* Edinburgh: Oliver and Boyd

Hoyle, E. 'The role of the change agent in educational innovation', in J. Walton (ed.) (1971), *Curriculum Organisation and Design,* London: Ward Lock Educational

Hoyle, E., 'The creativity of the school in Britain' in Harris, A., Lawn, M. and Prescott, W. (eds.) (1975), *Curriculum Innovation,* London: Croom Helm

Jackson, P. (1968), *Life in Classrooms,* New York: Holt, Rinehart and Winston

James, A. and Jeffcoate, R. (eds.) (1981), *The School in the Multicultural Society,* London: Harper and Row

James, M. and Ebbutt, D., 'Problems and potential', in J. Nixon (ed.) (1981), *A Teachers' Guide to Action Research,* London: Grant

McIntyre

Jeffcoate, R. (1979), *Positive Image: Towards a Multiracial Curriculum*, London: Writers and Readers Publishing Cooperative/Chameleon

Keddie, N. 'Classroom knowledge', in M. Young (ed.) (1971), *Knowledge and Control*, London: Collier-Macmillan

Keddie, N. (ed.) (1973), *Tinker, Tailor . . . The Myth of Cultural Deprivation*, Harmondsworth: Penguin

Kelly, A. (1982), *The Curriculum: Theory and Practice*, Second Edition, London: Harper and Row

Lacey, C. and Lawton, D. (eds.) (1981), *Issues in Evaluation and Accountability*, London: Methuen

Lawton, D., 'The idea of an integrated curriculum', in *Bulletin 19*, Autumn Term 1969, University of London Institute of Education

Lawton, D. (1973), *Social Change, Educational Theory and Curriculum Planning*, London: University of London Press

Lawton, D. (1975), *Class, Culture and the Curriculum*. London: Routledge and Kegan Paul

Lawton, D. (1980), *The Politics of the School Curriculum*, London: Routledge and Kegan Paul

Lobban, C., 'The influence of the school on sex-role typing', in J. Chetwynd and O. Hartnett (eds.) (1978), *The Sex Role System*, London: Routledge and Kegan Paul

Maclure, J. (1968a), *Curriculum Innovation in Practice*, London: HMSO

Maclure, J. (1968b), *Educational Documents, England and Wales, 1816–1968*, London: Methuen

MacDonald, B. and Walker, R. (1976), *Changing the Curriculum*, London: Open Books

MacDonald-Ross, M. (1973), 'Behavioural objectives: a critical review', in M. Golby, J. Greenwald and R. West (eds.) (1975), *Curriculum Design*, London: Croom Helm

Mager, R. (1962), *Preparing Instructional Objectives*, Palo Alto: Fearon

Mager, R. (1975), Second Edition

Meighan, R. (1981), *A Sociology of Educating*, Eastbourne: Holt, Rinehart and Winston

Merson, M. and Campbell, R., 'Community education: instruction for inequality', in *Education for Teaching*, No. 93, Spring 1974, ATDCE

Miles, M. (1965), 'Planned change and organisational health: figure and ground', in Harris, A., Lawn, M. and Prescott, W. (eds.) (1975), *Curriculum Innovation*, London: Croom Helm

Nixon, J. (ed.) (1981), *A Teachers' Guide to Action Research*, London: Grant McIntyre

Open University (1980), *Curriculum in Action: Practical Classroom Evaluation*. Blocks 1–4, Milton Keynes: Open University Press

Papert, S. (1980), *Mindstorms: Children, Computers and Powerful Ideas*, London: Harvester Press

Parlett, M. and Hamilton, D. (1972), 'Illuminative evaluation: a new approach to the study of innovatory programmes', in D. Hamilton *et al.* (eds.) (1977), *Beyond the Numbers Game*, London: Macmillan

Parsons, C. (1976), 'The new evaluation: a cautionary note; in R. McCormick (ed.) (1982), *Calling Education to Account*, London: Heinemann

Peters, R. (ed.) (1967), *The Concept of Education*, London: Routledge and Kegan Paul

Peters, R. (ed.) (1969), *Perspectives and Plowden*, London: Routledge and Kegan Paul

Phenix, P. (1964), *Realms of Meaning*, New York: McGraw Hill

Pidgeon, D. (1970), *Expectation and Pupil Performance*, Slough: NFER

Popham, W., 'Objectives and Instruction', in W. Popham, E. Eisner, H. Sullivan and L. Tyler (1969), *Instructional Objectives*, American Educational Research Association Monograph Series on Curriculum Evaluation, No. 3, Chicago: Rand McNally

Pring, R., 'Objectives and innovation: the irrelevance of theory', in London Educational Review, vol. 2, no. 3, Autumn 1973

Pring, R. (1976), *Knowledge and Schooling*, London: Open Books

Reid, W., 'The deliberative approach to the study of the curriculum and its relation to critical pluralism', in M. Lawn and L. Barton (eds.) (1981), *Rethinking Curriculum Studies*, London: Croom Helm

Schon, D. (1971), *Beyond the Stable State*, London: Temple Smith

Schools Council Research Studies (1973), *Pattern and Variation in Curriculum Development Projects: a Study of the Schools Council's Approach to Curriculum Development*, London: Macmillan

Schools Council Working Paper 42 (1972), *Education in the Middle Years*, London: Evans/Methuen

Schools Council Working Paper 53 (1975), *The Whole Curriculum 13–16*, London: Evans/Methuen

Schools Council Working Paper 55 (1975), *The Curriculum in the Middle Years*, London: Evans/Methuen

Schools Council Working Paper 70 (1981), *The Practical Curriculum*, London: Evans/Methuen

Schools Council Working Paper 75 (1983), *Primary Practice*, London: Evans/Methuen

Scriven, M., 'The methodology of evaluation', R. Stake, (ed.) (1967), *Perspectives of Curriculum Evaluation*, American Educational Research Association, Monograph on Curriculum Evaluation no. 1, Chicago: Rand McNally

Sharp, R. and Green, A. (1975), *Education and Social Control*, London: Routledge and Kegan Paul

Skilbeck, M., 'Strategies of curriculum change', in J. Walton, (ed.) (1971), *Curriculum Organisation and Design*, London: Ward Lock Educational

Skilbeck, M. (1972), 'School-based curriculum development', in J. Walton and J. Welton (eds.) (1976), *Rational Curriculum Planning: Four Case Studies*, London: Ward Lock Educational

Sockett, H., 'Behavioural objectives', in *London Educational Review*, vol. 2, no.3, Autumn 1975

Sockett, H. (ed.) (1980), *Accountability in the English Education System*, London: Hodder and Stoughton

Steadman, S. (1981), 'Evaluation techniques', in R. McCormick (ed.) (1982), *Calling Education to Account*, London: Heinemann

Stenhouse, L. (1975), *An Introduction to Curriculum Research and Development*, London: Heinemann

Stone, M. (1981), *The Education of the Black Child in Britain*, Glasgow: Fontana Paperbacks

Taylor, P. (1970), *How Teachers Plan their Courses*, Slough: NFER

Taylor, P., Reid, W., Holley B. and Exon, G. (1974), *Purpose, Power and Constraint in the Primary School Curriculum*, London: Macmillan

Tyler, R. (1949), *Basic Principles of Curriculum and Instruction*, Chicago: University of Chicago Press

Wastnedge, R., 'Whatever happened to Nuffield Junior Science?', in Unit 13 (1972), *Problems of Curriculum Innovation*, Open University Course E283, Bletchley: Open University Press

White, J. (1973), *Towards a Compulsory Curriculum*, London: Routledge and Kegan Paul

Whitfield, R., 'Curriculum objectives: help or hindrance?', in M. Golby (ed.) (1980), *Curriculum Change: The Lessons of a Decade*, Leicester University Press

Williams, R. 'An eclectic approach to evaluation', in C. Lacey and D. Lawton (eds.) (1981), *Issues in Evaluation and Accountability*, London: Routledge and Kegan Paul

Young, M., 'An approach to the study of curricula as socially organised knowledge', in M. Young (ed.) (1971), *Knowledge and Control*, London: Collier-Macmillan

Index